# CORRESPONDENCES

*An Anthology to Call for an End to Direct Provision*

edited by

**Stephen Rea and Jessica Traynor**

ISBN: 978-1-5272-4986-8



Cover design by Fintan Wall
www.fintanwall.com.

Typesetting by Benil Shah
www.webdprint.com

Printed by SPRINT-Print
Unit K9
Greenogue Business Park
Rathcoole,
Co. Dublin
Ireland.

First printing edition 2019.

Correspondences
21 Brookwood Rise
Artane
Dublin 5

Correspondencesanthology@gmail.com

# ACKNOWLEDGEMENTS

Thanks are due firstly to all the contributors who have given their time and creativity to this project.

Then to Stephen Rea and Professor Billy Hall who first approached me with this idea, and gave the support, both tangible and intangible, that made it happen.

Winter Song of the Guardian by Theo Dorgan first appeared in Nine Bright Shiners (Dedalus Press, 2014) and Home by Paula Meehan in Mysteries of the Home (Dedalus Press, 2013), reproduced here by kind permission of the authors and Dedalus Press.

Thanks to Fintan Wall for the beautiful cover design.

Thanks are also due to Pat Boran, Melatu Uche Okorie, Gráinne O'Toole, Skein Press, Paul Casey, Bulelani Mfaco, Lucky Khambule and all at MASI, Dr Natasha Remoundou, Margaret O'Brien, and Sarah Clancy.

This anthology has been made possible by a gift from The Atlantic Philanthropies Director/Employee Designated Gift Fund.

Last but never least, to my family.

Jessica Traynor

# TABLE OF CONTENTS

Acknowledgements ........ iii

Foreword ........ ix
*by Jessica Traynor*

Introduction ........ xi
*by Bulelani Mfaco*

Mother Tongue ........ 1
*by Mimmie Malaba*

Home ........ 2
*by Paula Meehan*

I Had to Keep On ........ 4
*by Anonymous*

Untitled ........ 8
*by Adam Wyeth*

Photography ........ 9
*by Heidar Al-Hashimi*

Note to Self ........ 11
*by Sarah Clancy*

(Hi)stories Contained: The Earl Grey Orphans Scheme, 1848–50 ........ 13
*by Dr Angela Byrne*

In Kabul I was Busy Playing ........ 21
*by Marwa Zamir*

For Marwa ........ 22
*by Claire Hennessy*

Never Again ........ 23
*by Donatien Francis*

Mentor's Note ........ 28
*by Christodoulos Makris*

La despedida ........ 29
*by Evgeny Shtorn*

They will come for you ........ 30
*by Evgeny Shtorn*

The body of my body ........ 31
*by Evgeny Shtorn*

Postscript ........ 32
*by Annemarie Ní Churreáin*

Because Justice Matters ........ 33
*by Anonymous*

Repeating the mistakes of the past ........ 37
*by Emilie Pine*

Visual art ........ 39
*by Hina Khan*

Philodendron ........ 42
*by Stephen Sexton*

Songs of Innocence, Songs of Experience ........ 43
*by Batur Nadir*

Workhouse ........ 49
*by Eileen Casey*

Borders ........ 50
*by Insaf Yalcinkaya*

A Worthless Life? ........ 53
*by Insaf Yalcinkaya*

Are You Proud? ........ 54
*by Insaf Yalcinkaya*

The Arrival of Shahmaran – with Apologies to St Patrick ........ 56
*by Katie Donovan*

Pain ........ 57
*by Nngcobo Bongamahlub*

At First Glance ........ 59
*by Nngcobo Bongamahlub*

Somewhere, Someone Else ........ 60
*by Elaine Feeney*

905976-14 .......... 62
*by Donnah Vuma*

An Inessential Journey .......... 66
*by Arnold Thomas Fanning*

Photography .......... 70
*by Vukašin Nedeljković*

In The Irish Countryside .......... 73
*by Dave Lordan*

An Emergency in Direct Provision .......... 78
*by Cónal Thomas*

Up The Hill In Mayo .......... 82
*by Owodunni Mustapha*

Managua to Finglas .......... 84
*by Jane Clarke*

Behind the Wall I Escape .......... 85
*by Deborah Oniah Blankson*

Winter Song Of The Guardian .......... 87
*by Theo Dorgan*

What's in a Name? .......... 88
*by Rehan Ali*

Endless Summer .......... 90
*by Ian Maleney*

The Welcoming Project .......... 92
*by Catherine Young*

Scars .......... 95
*by Nokukhanya Dlamini*

Scalpel .......... 96
*by Jessica Traynor*

Biographies .......... 97

# Foreword

## by Jessica Traynor

A few years ago, I sat at the dinner table in my parents' house, asking my Dad, a Finglas native born in the 1950s, what he had known as a child about the industrial school at Artane. He recalled that there was almost a glamour around the boys, but a dangerous glamour – they were separated from society for some reason that wasn't clear. But it had something to do with difference, with badness. And the threat of being sent to Artane was one he heard spoken by parents to their children all the way through his own childhood.

That afternoon I speculated on what my own children might ask me about when they were old enough to start tangling with history, society, and what is silenced.

My father was a child of de Valera's Ireland, of McQuaid's Ireland. He grew up in a working class area, in a society which had been indoctrinated by a conjoined church and state into believing that incarceration – of women in Magdalene Laundries, of children in Industrial Schools and Mother and Baby Homes, of people suffering from mental illness in asylums – was for for the benefit of society.

I did not grow up in this Ireland. I grew up in the 1980s and 90s, when old certainties were slowly, grindingly being eroded and in some wonderful cases, being swept away.

And yet. In 2000, direct provision was introduced as a temporary measure to process migrants seeking international protection. Almost twenty years later, this carceral system is still in place. As a citizen of the state, how do I explain this? How will I explain my silence to my children?

During Field Day's *Right to Have Rights* lecture series in 2017-18, I was invited by Stephen Rea to read some of my poetry which responds to the direct provision system. I read alongside poets in direct provision such as Christiana Obaro, and members of new Irish communities such as Chiamaka Enyi-Amadi. I listened to Seamus Deane tackle Hannah Arendt's seminal *Eichmann in Jerusalem: A Report on the Banality of Evil* and Judge Bryan MacMahon discuss the recommendations of the MacMahon report. Afterwards, myself, Stephen, and Professor Billy Hall, a physician who has worked with both children and adults in direct provision centres and who clinically advises organizations providing specialized medical care for such individuals, discussed what we in our disparate fields might do to continue the conversation.

The idea for Correspondences was born through discussion with activists and artists in the field, all of whom gave sage and practical advice. We were keen not to simply ghettoise work in an ephemeral anthology that would create short term engagement with artists and writers in direct provision, and short term results. We also wanted to benefit a charity run by and for those who have experience as applicants for international protection, and so choose MASI as the beneficiary of the proceeds of the anthology. We wanted to pair artists and writers in the system with Irish writers for mentorship opportunities, in the hope that these working relationships and friendships would outlast the process of the anthology itself. In this process of pairing artists, we were led by the submissions we received from writers, photographers and visual artists in direct provision, pairing them with mentors or other writers according to the needs and interests of each individual artist. We were also approached by a number of commentators, historians, artists and activists who wished to contribute something on their own experience working with people in direct provision, and so we commissioned a number of essays to record their experience.

But mostly, we hoped to create empathy, and connections, and understanding, between a misunderstood and sometimes demonised community, made up of diverse people with complex lives, and the people who have the privilege to live in the Irish state without fear, without suspicion, and without prejudice.

In the vast span of history, as we discover more and more about the evolutionary process of humankind, in this deep, deep history where facts, figures and statistics can obliterate our emotional connection to our ancestors, there are secluded instances that spark recognition. Cup shaped depressions hammered into the rock in the Bhimbetka Caves between 700,000 and 290,000 BCE. The Venus of Tan-Tan, a feminine form carved in pre-Homo Sapiens between 500,000 and 200,000 BCE. The El Castillo Cave paintings of 39,000 BCE, a collection of linear animal drawings and hand prints potentially left by our Homo Sapiens ancestors. All of these marks make a statement that transcends language and cultural difference: 'I am here. Remember me.'

This is what art does. It serves as a reminder of humanity, of connection, of lived experience. We hope that these poems, essays and personal records of the experiences of people in direct provision in Ireland at the beginning of the 21st century, paired with the heartfelt responses of Irish writers to their fellow men and women, might serve as a much-needed reminder of the transformative joys of empathy. And I hope it might serve as the start of a story of change that I and all involved in the project will be proud to tell to future generations.

# Introduction

BY BULELANI MFACO

In the autumn of 2014, something extraordinary happened. Asylum seekers who were fed up with unbearable conditions in Kinsale Road Direct Provision Centre (officially Kinsale Road Accommodation Centre) raised their fists of defiance, resistance, solidarity and conviction. They blocked the main entrance and prevented staff from entering.

One of the founders of MASI (the Movement of Asylum Seekers in Ireland), Lucky Khambule, says they had several meetings in the weeks before the protests. A resolution to stage a protest was passed. On the morning of the protest in Kinsale Road Direct Provision Centre, the mood changed from that of an obedient asylum seeker at the mercy of an Aramark Manager (who, in Seneliso Mkoko's words, exudes prisoner-jailer attitude when working with residents), to a strong, courageous and defiant asylum seeker.

They woke up in that morning and lined up at the main entrance to Kinsale Road Direct Provision Centre to prevent Aramark staff from entering. The residents had formed committees to do work that is ordinarily done by Aramark staff. The cooking committee was tasked with ensuring that no one went hungry during the lockout.

On a different day of the lockout, a black couch, common in many direct provision centres, was placed in the middle of the road to block the driveway. Asylum seekers sat on the couch. Lucky Khambule has fond memories of how different the mood was in the centre for the 10 days staff were locked out. He recalls that for the first time people felt a sense of freedom as there was no manager or staff to infantilise them.

That protest sent a message to the Irish government that asylum seekers were not going to be quiet anymore. The women, men, and children who made placards and blocked the entrance to the Kinsale Road Direct Provision Centre reclaimed a political space that had long been occupied by NGOs advocating for asylum seekers. It sent a message to them that asylum seekers can actually speak. If there is one thing to be learned from Kinsale Road Direct Provision Centre residents, it's the need to listen to people who are deliberately placed on the margins of Irish society. When they speak, it comes with a lot of pain and takes courage. Pain because of the situations people have been through prior to reaching Irish shores, and courage because of the experience of having to live in the abhorrent system of direct provision.

It has always been difficult to complain in direct provision. When asylum seekers protested in Mosney Direct Provision Centre in April this year, the owner is recorded as threatening the asylum seekers. He suggested that their protest would have an impact on their applications for international protection. Similarly in Portsalon, coordinator Lucky Khambule met with frightened women in August this year. They told him that the owner of Portsalon House Emergency Direct Provision Centre in County Donegal had threatened them with deportation after they complained and that two women asylum seekers who lived there were moved to Cork to silence them. The biggest fear in every asylum seeker is that their application will be rejected and they will be deported after that. Threats of deportation exacerbate mental health issues which is a big problem in direct provision, with many asylum seekers taking sleeping pills or antidepressants which only serve to numb the trauma. The owner threatening vulnerable women with deportation when they live in a very isolated village is incredibly cruel.

Complaining and protesting against the appalling conditions asylum seekers are expected to live in can be met with such cruelties. The asylum seekers I met when I went to Dunkerrin Arms Emergency Direct Provision Centre in County Offaly are expected to be happy with the owner serving them lunch at 3:38pm. I asked the owner if he was serving dinner and he said it is lunch. Can you imagine starving for hours, not having money, in the middle of nowhere, completely at the mercy of a greedy owner of an emergency Direct Provision centre who will show up at 3:38pm with rice and fries for lunch and expect you to be happy and grateful for it?

Another owner of an emergency Direct Provision centre imposed a 10pm curfew on adult asylum seeking men in the Central Hostel in County Clare. This illustrates the controlling and dehumanising treatment asylum seekers are subjected to. And it also underscores the courage of the Kinsale Road Direct Provision Centre residents who shut the place down for 10 days. All their placards had messages that raised the core issues they had with direct provision. A young boy carried a placard with 'Born in Ireland. 9 years in limbo. Are we different from others?' to highlight the length of time people spend in direct provision waiting for a decision on their asylum claim. Another placard had 'Save us from depression. Give us back our lives' on it.

This is the limbo asylum seekers are subjected to, where days become weeks, weeks become months, and months become years, waiting for a letter from the Department of Justice and Equality. It has an enormous impact on the mental health of asylum seekers. You Jung Han, a young woman from South Korea claimed asylum in Ireland with her 6-year-old child in 2015. She, like most asylum seekers, had mental health problems. People who claim asylum have already been through traumatic experiences. And being stripped of personal autonomy, dignity, and forced to watch people live their lives, doing all the things you are not allowed to do, compounds that pre-migration trauma. You Jung Han had hope for sanctuary when she came to Ireland. And hope that her fundamental rights would not be undermined here. In August 2016, her little boy was out playing with his friend in Kinsale Road Direct Provision Centre. The 6-year-old boy returned from playing with his friend, knocked in the room and there was no answer. After knocking for a while, the boy and his friend went to security guards to get them to open the room. On opening the room, the security guard found You Jung Han dead. She hanged herself in her room, two years after the protest where concerns about mental health were raised by asylum seekers. Tusla took her child in their care and her family may never know what happened to their daughter. If this tells us anything about the response to the protest in Kinsale Road Direct Provision Centre it's that the government did not address the core issues that were raised by the courageous asylum seekers who led the protest action.

You Jung Han is not the last person to die through suicide in Direct Provision. In March 2019, Mussie, a young man from Eritrea hanged himself from a tree near the Hazel Hotel Direct Provision Centre in County Kildare. The Department of Justice and Equality knew that there were traumatised asylum seekers they were sending there before the centre was opened. They asked the Health Services Executive (HSE) to send their mental health staff. Their mental health expert visited the Hazel Hotel Direct Provision Centre. The expert went back to the Department of Justice and Equality and said "let them cook," as if cooking addresses trauma. Months later, Mussie hanged himself in the centre that had recently installed self-catering facilities for asylum seekers. This is indicative of the inappropriate responses or remedies employed by the Irish government when it comes to vindicating the rights of asylum seekers. They had to be dragged to the highest court in Ireland to allow asylum seekers to work. Now they expect to be applauded for allowing asylum seekers to cook, one of the most basic of human activities. Perhaps the Irish State should reflect on why NGOs and a judge are praising them for allowing asylum seekers to cook. Much of MASI's work is to end the abhorrent system of direct provision as all evidence shows that it strips human beings basic rights such as cooking, working, and pursuing their ambitions. And the system subjects asylum seekers to petty bureaucratic processes and hotel and B&B managers who have no idea how to work with vulnerable people.

At the core of our campaign is the need to claim and assert our right to live as free human beings. This means seeing asylum seekers as human beings worthy of respect and dignity. And human beings have talents that must be allowed to, and given space to flourish. The asylum seekers who contributed to this anthology have done just that. They have shown that they are talented and without the structural barriers imposed on their lives by the State, they could do more to contribute to this country through the arts, activism and just by being human beings pursuing happiness. And that can only happen when direct provision is abolished along with the legal and structural barriers that prevent asylum seekers from doing all the things human beings do.

August 2019

# Mother Tongue

BY MIMMIE MALABA

My language is as thick as my mother's
it was passed down to me like the curves
of my sharp Xs and j-like expressions on Ys
now carried over the seas slowly forgetting expressions
my tongue is as sharp as a two edged sword
it can slice you to bits without you even noticing the brutal I –
barbeque that I slay when it's meant to be BBQ
my language is the diviner of roads
knocking on the knock knock beetle
as I crack open the clicks on my tongue
Irqika lendlela luqoqothwane
I was bred by deep souls of culture
so engraved in my blood refusing to deteriorate
like my name Minenhle
the beautiful afternoon that people turn down
because of their ungifted unsharp tongues
they don't know that I climb up over mountains as spirits flow out
I am a knock knock beetle
I am after all my mother's daughter
the road's imigwaqo
the traffic light's robots
the flows of my qa qe qi qo qus –
are the chewings of xhaku xhaku
and the spitting out of seeds from people
undeserving of my mother tongue?

# Home

BY PAULA MEEHAN

I am the blind woman finding her way home by a map of tune.
When the song that is in me is the song I hear from the world
I'll be home. It's not written down and I don't remember the words.
I know when I hear it I'll have made it myself. I'll be home.

A version I heard once in Leitrim was close, a wet Tuesday night
in the Sean Relig bar. I had come for the session, I stayed
for the vision and lore. The landlord called time,
the music dried up, the grace notes were pitched to the dark.
When the jukebox blared out *I'd only four senses and he left me senseless*,
I'd no choice but to take to the road. On Grafton Street in November
I heard a mighty sound: a travelling man with a digeridoo
blew me clear to Botany Bay. The tune too far back to live in
but scribed on my bones. In a past life I may have been Kangaroo,
rocked in my dreamtime, convict ships coming o'er the foam.

In the Puzzle Factory one winter I was sure I was home.
The talking in tongues, the riddles, the rhymes, struck a chord
that cut through the pharmaceutical haze. My rhythm catatonic,
I lulled myself back to the womb, my mother's heart
beating the drum of herself and her world. I was tricked
by her undersong, just close enough to my own. I took then
to dancing; I spun like a Dervish. I swear I heard the subtle
music of the spheres. It's no place to live — but,
out there in space, on your own hung aloft the night.
The tune was in truth a mechanical drone;
I was a pitiful monkey jigging on cue. I came back to earth
with a land, to rain on my face, to sun in my hair. And grateful too.

The wisewomen say you must live in your skin, call *it* home,
no matter how battered or broken, misused by the world, you can heal.
This morning a letter arrived on the nine o'clock post:
The Department of Historical Reparation and who did I blame?
The Nuns? Your Mother? The State? *Tick box provided,*
*we'll consider your case.* I'm burning my soapbox, I'm taking
the very next train. A citizen of nowhere, nothing to my name.

I'm on my last journey. Though my lines are all wonky
they spell me a map that makes sense. Where the song that is in me
is the song I hear from the world, I'll set down my burdens
and sleep. The spot that I lie on at last the place I'll call home.

# I Had to Keep On

BY ANONYMOUS

As narrated by an Afghan man to Dr Natasha Remoundou

## Foreword

This is his story exactly as he told it. In late April 2019 he narrated to me his journey from Afghanistan to Ireland and asked me to write it down on paper. I had been trying for a long time to convince him that his story mattered too and had to be heard and read. He finally accepted. These are his words, his rhythm, his memories, his sentences, his pauses, his full stops, and his ellipses while he was verbally recounting his steps since the day he had to escape from his country, Afghanistan, and set off on his 21st century forced odyssey, a teenager in flight. My duty has been primarily to listen to what he wanted to say and appreciate his deep trust. I felt I had to be fully present in the moment while his haunting account of a long and perilous journey from Asia to Europe through the Mediterranean Sea unfolded as a summary of human survival, resilience, and hope across borders and continents. Sitting there listening to him after our English class in the big square room in a direct provision centre in rural Ireland felt somewhat surreal and confusing. For here we were, in the relative safety of a room, in a democratic country, in a provincial town, on the farthest side of Europe, thousands of miles away from this man's Afghan village where he lived for most of his young life. We are now in Europe, but are we really living in safety and with dignity enjoying basic human rights? Is Ireland, the final destination, a home, an Ithaca of sorts? And are there ears to listen to these stories of unwilling stasis and denied mobility and hands to write them down, and eyes to read them and reverberate their message? As I write this introduction, I am reminded of the mission of this publication, Correspondences, and that in our privilege of freedom of movement we have a duty to act as intermediaries, a sort of modern day scribe of stories of refugee survivors, many of whom are children collecting institutionalized childhood memories in a perpetual state of waiting in direct provision, so that they are recorded, archived, memorialized, scrutinized. With a recorder in hand and an impatient and hungry baby, my daughter, on my lap, we began: I followed him and his comrades through a kaleidoscope, past mountains and dinghy boats traversing the Aegean, till they reached my city, Athens, seeking asylum. I was hoping that in his very short stay there he would have found one single hospitable person among my own people, some help and comfort he and so many refugees desperately seek when they flee home in search of a safer life. Along endless railways, boats, trucks and parallel yet different private stories of migration, we meet in Ireland. Perhaps, we all have more than one Ithaca to return to after all. This is his story.

Dr Natasha Remoundou

"That morning the Taliban broke into our house. They beat me and my mother so bad and locked us in a bedroom. My father was not at home as he was in the army. We stayed in the room locked and terrified till night fell and then one of the Taliban unlocked the door and we escaped. We escaped with my mother. I was so badly injured that I had to go to the hospital. I thought my injuries were not that serious but when I went to the hospital I got stitches on my head. I was only 16 years old. Then my mother talked to someone and I escaped the country by car. The Afghan driver was unknown to me and he drove me to Pakistan. My mother had arranged everything so that I would be saved. My mother stayed behind. They killed her. Still to this day, I do not know where my father is. In Pakistan, I had an aunt who lived there with her family. She is my mother's sister. When I went to Pakistan I stayed in the hospital for three weeks because I was bleeding on my head. Then, my aunt told me that I had to leave the country. I was posing a threat to her own family and her husband was not happy with me staying with them. They were afraid that they would be in trouble as they were looking for me.

I crossed the borders again with a group of people. My aunt and her husband found people to take me out of the country. So, I left Pakistan and crossed again the borders with a group of other people and reached Iran. I stayed there for a year. It was very tough there. I did not know anyone there and it was very difficult my time there. I met a few Afghan people – most of them illegal – who gave me a place to stay and I worked for a year sewing clothes for very little money. I could not complain because I was illegally in the country and if I got caught they would deport me to Syria. There were only two options available for me if I got caught: either to go join the army and fight in Syria in the war or go back to my country Afghanistan. So, because I had not legal documents, I could be forced to go fight in Syria or go back to Afghanistan. I have a lot of friends who were coerced and recruited to become Hazara (Shi'a) fighters. I did not want to do this.

From Iran I walked with a group of people through the mountains to Turkey and from there we took a boat to Mytilini, an island in Greece. We tried a few times to reach the shore. I saw people drowning. From the 50 people we set off with only 15 of us made it to Mytilini. I don't know how to swim. Even people wearing vests drowned.

In Mytilini 20 or 30 of us got arrested by the police and we were put to jail for six to seven months. But I was lucky. You can stay for up to two years in prison for no reason. Just for crossing the borders. Just because you are a refugee. After I was released from prison I was given a document stating that I had one month to leave the country. If within this month you fail to do so, they put you back to prison or they deport you back to your country of origin. I was broke and knew no one there. It was difficult to leave Greece. From Mytilini, I borrowed money and took a ferry to Piraeus. Once I arrived in Athens I had no connections. If you don't make friends you have problems. And that is the same everywhere. Greece is a beautiful country but I didn't like it there. There is a lot of racism. A large group of people, around 50 of them, would attack you in squares wearing black T-shirts and balaclavas. This never happened to me but to my friend. I never went out at night time. I used to live in the city centre, in Acharnon, near a church. I made a friend who helped me when I was there. After a month I had to leave Greece. So, I left Athens and went to Thessaloniki and from there I started walking. It was winter time.

There was no snow but it was freezing cold and it rained heavily. My feet were soaked and cold. My clothes were wet from the constant rain. I was walking for hours when I saw a bridge and a railway line on a rocky area. There were huge rocks around me. My feet were swollen and bleeding. I went under the bridge. All my clothes were soaked wet but I was carrying a sleeping bag in my backpack. I had no other choice but to sleep there as I was exhausted. I took all my clothes off and remained naked in that foreign landscape in the cold and got in my sleeping back. Only a few minutes passed when I started shivering from the freezing cold. My body could not stop shaking. My eyelids were closing. One thing kept coming to my mind: that if I allowed myself to fall sleep I would die. I said *No. You have to wake up.* I got out of my sleeping bag, put my wet, cold clothes back on and said to myself that I had to keep on walking. I walked for three more kilometres. There was no other option or choice. I had to walk. I found a police station and wanted to be caught and sent back. Then I would have 10 days to cross the border again. Indeed, they sent me back.

Ten days later I prepared myself again for crossing the Greek borders. With new clothes, new shoes, a new bag. I decided to take the same route. The way I knew. Following the railways. Only this time I was not on my own. I was part of a group of refugees all of us crossing the borders out of Greece together. We were strangers but all there for a common journey. That journey was not easier the second time round. A father and a son were crushed by a train inside a tunnel. I heard their cries that last moment. It was on the border with Macedonia. When you were in a train tunnel you had to position your body in a certain way to avoid being crushed by the train.

The rest of us carried on. We reached Kosovo and then Serbia. In Macedonia, Albanians robbed us. They took our mobile phones, our clothes, our shoes, watches, wallets. Then we crossed to Serbia. Then we reached Hungary. There it was so bad: Hungarian police were so racist. There I had no clothes. I found a pair of girls' flip-flops in the garbage. They were very small on my feet but had to wear them. The Hungarian police gave us nothing. I was wearing a woman's leggings. I found clothes and shoes on the street. I had no other choice. We ate what we found from our friends. No locals ever offered us food. We carried no weapons with us. Then we went to the prison in Hungary on the borders of the country. I could not walk any more as I had severe blisters. I stayed in a camp there for two weeks for my feet to heal. From there we had to keep walking. We reached France. We found ourselves in the Calais refugee camp. From there we hid inside trucks for days to reach Ireland. I got inside the top of a truck. In some trucks there could be as many as 10 people hiding. They caught me a few times hiding in trucks. They start spraying and refugees come out. From Calais I reached finally Dublin after a 20-hour trip. From there I was put in direct provision. And here I am.

# Untitled

BY ADAM WYETH

The woman who runs the charity shop
says she feels she's given birth to me.
All those years in my country
I was a gestating egg amorphous as the night.

Now here I am
limbs and head
a recently arrived émigré.

I lock the shop and watch it grow small
    and dark.
I feel like a drone circling above
as someone thumbs the controls.

My whole life
        could fall
         through their fingers
      in a matter
of seconds.

I am plunging towards the city lights
the tall buildings rise up like sharp teeth.
I don't know if I'm at the beginning
or coming to an end.

An unbroken stream of people rush past.
Am I a stone in the middle of the river
or a river constantly in contact with the stone?

There is a book in the shop
yet to be picked up
it stands on the shelf waiting
for eyes        to give it sight
and tongue    to give it breath.

# Photography

BY HEIDAR AL-HASHIMI

33
32

# Note to Self

BY SARAH CLANCY

look at fence, wall, checkpoint, detention centre
look at wire, breeze block, sheet metal,
look at sandbags, concrete road-blocks and portacabins
look at reinforced glass and interlocking door systems
consider that the factories that made them
are all staffed by humans and how it took others to erect them
in our specially selected zones of exclusion
and that on some level those people
knew what they were doing

think of small components for very large weapons
how someone dreamed up each piece of them
and check out our latest technological solutions
for the crisis of humans only moving from one place to another
watch a human resource put their night vision goggles on securely
and check their thermal imaging system
for the outline of something warm and human
on the shift where they clock out clock in to an automated system
remember no camp could exist
without people to build it

look at legislation and its deceptions
where international protection
means much swifter deportations and indefinite detention
where everything is a metaphor for something,
look at getting a handcuffed person on a plane
to extradite them and see that a second person
is on the sweet end of those handcuffs
and has no particular meretricious distinction
except for those invented by officialdom
to make them feel different, so they can do
what would otherwise be unthinkable

remember that someone starts that plane and flies it
and before that some yawning human rubber-stamped
the letter to warn application number 237

that someone was coming to get them
and then went home to take their own children swimming
and before that again some other person in an office
deliberated about a place that they had never visited
that they wouldn't be seen dead in
and determined that it was a safe country
in the legal definition
as if that meant anything
remember that there's never been a wall
that someone didn't build
or a border that was anything but abstract,
think about how there's never been a noose that no-one fashioned
and remember that on both ends
of all this all this infrastructure there are only humans;
it is us that's doing this.

# (Hi)stories Contained: The Earl Grey Orphans Scheme, 1848–50

by Dr Angela Byrne

In December 1848, the *Earl Grey* docked in Sydney harbour carrying 217 Irish teenage girls who had buried two of their companions at sea. This launched the 'Earl Grey orphans' scheme which, over a two-year period, saw the removal of 4,114 teenage girls from 119 Irish workhouses to the Australian colonies as part of the British government's response to chronic workhouse overcrowding during the Great Famine of 1847–52. These teenagers were among the estimated two million people who left Ireland in the years 1845–55. The scheme – like today's direct provision system – can be understood as part of a long culture of containment, whereby those on the fringes of 'mainstream' Irish life have been institutionalised.

Selected for their good health and character, the girls were on average aged sixteen when they began their new lives in the distant colonies. The regimen of workhouse life continued during the long sea voyage, where they were closely monitored by the ship's surgeon, who made formal reports to colonial immigration authorities. However, the confined teenagers made a vulnerable cargo. The sexual abuse of several Dublin girls aboard the *Subraon* in 1849 was understood in terms of the girls' own moral laxity, despite the fact that they had been intoxicated by their abusers, and despite the tragic death of one Dolly Newman by haemorrhage, likely due to miscarriage. Officials emphasised that some of the girls 'pursu[ed] at Sydney the evil courses into which they had been initiated on the voyage by the captain and his officers.'

Upon arrival in Sydney, the girls were housed in Hyde Park immigration depot, a former prison and the third stage of their containment. There, they spent their days performing chores and receiving visits from clergy, nuns and medical officers, while awaiting the offer of an apprenticeship or indentured servitude, often to live by harsh rules and at the mercy of their employer.

The 'Irish orphans' attracted disproportionate criticism from the colonists. Australian newspapers took a sensationalist approach when any of the girls came to public attention; Melbourne's *Argus* newspaper was particularly critical. Much of the negative publicity reflected anti-Catholic sentiment, and unfounded fears that the girls would be a drain on colonial resources. In the fledgling Australian colonies, men outnumbered women three-to-one, creating particular demand for domestic servants and wives. The majority of the girls married within three years of arrival, realising, as stated in the *Sydney Morning Herald* on 11 July 1850, 'the great object with which they had been introduced.' Some made marriages that improved their material standard of living, but others suffered domestic violence, as recorded in the Australian courts.

Despite the occasional defence of migration, particularly against the backdrop of the Great Famine, negative publicity forced the discontinuation of the scheme in 1850. However, as the final extract demonstrates, the culture of containment continued, with immigrants being placed in the same inhumane conditions in other colonial immigration depots for years to come. Historic containments cannot yet be spoken of in the past tense. The parallels between the 'Earl Grey orphans' and residents in direct provision today are many and obvious, but the key features bear repeating in the context of today's soaring global displacement figures. In the absence of choice, they exercised agency; under the eye and regimen of the state, abuses were perpetrated; then as now, populist discourse fuelled mistrust.

The following extracts are quoted directly from nineteenth-century newspapers.

*Sydney Morning Herald*, 30 September 1848
HYDE PARK BARRACKS. – The convict barracks, in Hyde Park, have been handed over to the Colonial Government … the large wards on the upper floors will be fitted up as quarters for the Irish orphans upon their first arrival.

*Sydney Morning Herald*, 19 October 1848
FEMALE ORPHANS BY THE EARL GREY.
PERSONS desiring to obtain servants or apprentices from amongst the female orphans who have arrived in the Earl Grey, are requested to send in written applications for the same …

It will be understood that in accordance with the general rule which has been for some time observed by the Government in the disposal of Female Immigrants, the orphans placed under the charge of the Committee will not be allowed to accept situations in inns or other houses of public entertainment.

The orphans will be landed, and lodged in the Institution at Hyde Park, where, on some future day, of which due intimation will be given, they may be inspected by such applicants under this notice as shall have been approved of by the Committee.

FRANCIS L.S. MEREWETHER,
Agent for Immigration, and Chairman of the Orphan Immigration Committee.

*Sydney Morning Herald*, 2 October 1849
FEMALE APPRENTICES. – It is to be regretted that complaints are generally on the increase against orphan girls, who have arrived and been apprenticed; although it is but just to say that for some months they conducted themselves (with a very few exceptions) to the satisfaction of their employers, but many of them appear to grow "weary of well doing." … the girls seem to have found out, that the only punishment awarded for disobedience, is that of cancelling the indentures, and returning them to barracks, where they make sure of meeting some of their old companions, and also stand a chance of seeing some other part of the colony.

*Sydney Morning Herald*, 4 January 1850
STATE OF THE IMMIGRATION DEPOT ON THE 1ST JANUARY. – Number of persons who arrived as prisoners' families by the ship Success, 71. Immigrants who arrived by the ships Panama and William Jardine, 29; Irish orphans who arrived by the ship Inchinnan, 5. Total, 105.
…

IRISH ORPHAN GIRL. – Frances Tearnen, apprenticed to Mr. John Kennedy, appeared before their Worships, Mr. Hardy, P.M., and Dr. Anderson, J.P. The girl's behaviour before the Bench clearly indicated her character. Mrs. Kennedy deposed that the girl was impudent in the extreme … showing her mistress sundry five-shilling pieces, stating she had received them from single men; also, that Frances had expressed her determination to be married, and be her own mistress. Mr. Kennedy stated he could not keep the girl, and the indentures were cancelled.

*Sydney Morning Herald*, 18 January 1850
IRISH ORPHAN GIRLS. – … Ellen Welch, apprenticed to Mr. George Wentworth of Greendale, near Penrith, appeared before the Court, dressed in the latest fashions, her face was encircled with artificial flowers of the most choice selection, and her general appearance was certainly not that of a servant. Her master said she was insolent, refused to do her work, and attempted to assault her mistress. … The indentures were cancelled, and she returned to Barracks.

*The Goulburn Herald and County of Argyle Advertiser*, 2 February 1850
There are upwards of 400 of those "dear girls" the Irish orphans, remaining disengaged at the depot at Hyde Park Barracks.

*Bell's Life in Sydney and Sporting Reviewer*, 16 February 1850
The Irish Orphan Girls are going the whole hog at Parramatta. Mary Phillips, one of them, has been committed to take her trial for stabbing a fellow-servant, Andrew Jones, in the groin
…

*Sydney Morning Herald*, 19 February 1850
IRISH ORPHAN GIRLS.

*To the Editors of the Sydney Morning Herald.*
GENTLEMEN, – Some of your correspondents seem to take a peculiar pleasure in finding out and publishing every fault or defect of character, that may appear in these helpless victims of a "national calamity." To every generous mind they ought to be objects of compassion and kind consideration. … They are hired expressly for the purpose of being *instructed* in domestic service, as the very term of being "apprenticed" clearly indicates. You, gentlemen, could not expect an "apprentice" in your office to set up a column of type without committing many faults and blunders, perhaps for the first twelve months …

There is a certain species of mental obliquity prevalent in some British colonies, and occasionally very rife in New South Wales, which may be called "Hiberno-Phobia." I think some of your "Correspondents" must have been labouring under this disease when penning their very bitter invectives against these poor Irish Orphans. …

I remain, Gentlemen,
Your obedient servant,
FAIR PLAY.

*Sydney Morning Herald*, 1 March 1850
IRISH ORPHAN GIRLS.
*To the Editors of the Sydney Morning Herald.*

GENTLEMEN, – Two letters have recently appeared in your paper on the above subject, on which one or two remarks may not be out of place.
…

Another of your correspondents complained of what he was pleased to call "*Hiberno-phobia.*" I think he would have more accurately described this as *Romano-phobia.* Such of our citizens as walk upon Hyde Park are constantly exposed to this feeling being stirred up. Everybody remarks on the regiment of these girls which is constantly marched into the Romish Chapel; and there is at least one half of our population who are irritated that out of the 1300 orphan girls who have been imported at public expense, more than 1100 have been Roman Catholics. If we transplant Tipperary to New South Wales, we know full well that we shall have its habits with its people, and as the police have quite enough to do already, we don't want this. …

A LOOKER ON.
February 28, 1850.

*Sydney Morning Herald*, 8 July 1850
IRISH ORPHANS. – There are at present three hundred and fifty of these girls in the Hyde Park Barracks (all but four of them Roman Catholics), and the Tippoo Saib is daily expected with about three hundred more.

*Sydney Morning Herald*, 11 July 1850
[Mr Donaldson of the Legislative Council addresses the Colonial Secretary.] … In the disposal of their own money, he had always said the colonists were unfairly treated. … One proof of this was that they were deluged with Irish orphan immigration – not for the benefit of the colony, but to relieve the poor-law unions of Ireland. … Why that at this present moment 390 of these girls, against whom he wished to say nothing but that they were not fit and serviceable immigrants, were suffering durance vile, were immured in a kind of modern Bastile, known as Hyde Park Barracks.
…

[Mr Murray responds.] … There was one remark of the honourable member for Durham which, as an Irishman, he felt bound to allude. The hon gentleman, according to the fashion of the day, had alluded in terms of censure to the system of orphan emigration from Ireland. The whole of these censures were without the slightest foundation – for the conduct of these females was as correct in every particular as that of immigrants from any other part of the British dominions.

It might be true that they were not very efficient servants in the luxurious establishments of the metropolis, but they were well fitted to become wives and mothers, and latter was the great object with which they had been introduced.
…

The ATTORNEY-GENERAL defended the class of female immigrants, known as Irish orphans. He believed they were as respectable as any other class of servants, nor was it from any misconduct of theirs that there happened to be a large number of them in the Immigration Depôt just at present. It was simply, because a large number had arrived during the last week.

*Freeman's Journal*, 11 July 1850
IRISH ORPHAN GIRLS.
…

The most shameful and groundless charge of immorality made against the Orphans by the *Argus*, and re-echoed by the City Council of Melbourne, has been taken up and most triumphantly refuted by the Irish residents in Port Phillip. … Wherever any of them have fallen, it has been the work of seduction or violence. We have received satisfactory information from several respectable parties in the interior, as to the general good character of the Orphans in their localities. We freely admit that the majority of them are not thorough servants, but in general they are, honest, sober and hardworking, three qualities not always found united in the female servants of New South Wales.
…

The *Herald* complains of the expense of supporting these girls for a few weeks at Hyde Park Barracks, but these expenses are small when compared to the benefit that the public derive from having a sufficient supply of female servants at hand, and that at reduced wages. No, neither the expenses, nor the pretended uselessness of these girls, is the real cause of the outcry against them, but it is because they are under the "curse," of which Dean Swift so bitterly complains — they were born in *Ireland* … Many of the Orphans have reason to complain of the many impediments thrown in their way to prevent them from attending their place of worship, although this is expressly provided for in their Indentures — this sours their temper and then they become sullen, and indifferent to the fulfilment of their duties, and then new causes of complaint arise ... We have dwelt rather long upon this disagreeable subject, but we were anxious to remove from the public mind some part of the prejudice which has been excited against these unoffending Orphans; and to point out the real cause of that prejudice.

*Sydney Morning Herald*, 17 July 1850
ORPHAN IMMIGRATION.
Mr. OAKES moved that an Address be presented to His Excellency the Governor, praying that he will be pleased to cause to be laid on the table of this House, a return showing the undermentioned particulars respecting the Female Orphan Emigration ... there was a great difference of opinion prevailing upon this matter, which rendered the publication of some authentic data necessary.

The COLONIAL SECRETARY would have felt better satisfied if the honorable member had stated more explicitly the object for which he sought this information. It was not however, his intention to offer any opposition to the giving of these returns. ... The total cost of importing these females had been ... about £12 8s. per head. The cost of maintaining the orphans in Hyde Park Barracks did not amount to more than 3d. each per diem. There were at present 353 in this establishment – but of this number 228 arrived very recently in the Maria. The remaining 39 were girls whose indentures had been cancelled for various reasons by the magistrates in Petty Sessions. ... In March last, the Committee at Sydney, referred to the very large immigration of Irish orphans which had taken place, and unanimously resolved that a strong recommendation should be made to the government, that the emigration of female orphans from the workhouses in Ireland should for the present be discontinued. This recommendation was accordingly made by the Governor in a despatch dated 22nd April last. The opinion of both Committees appeared to be, that the female orphans who have arrived have been, with a few exceptions, as would be expected, well conducted; that for certain description of service they are well suited; but that they should not be sent to the colony in very great numbers, and that the passages of such as are sent should be partly paid for by the parishes from which they come.

*Argus*, 21 August 1857
THE IMMIGRATION DEPOT.

… though in most respects the Depot is seemingly well managed, there is not, and especially in the married people's wards, due provision for either cleanliness or decency.

… There are no lavatories for either men or women. Immigrants are supposed to bring their own basins, and there are tubs of water for the supply of all who choose to take it; but men and women must perform the scanty ablutions possible in public.

… In saying this, we by no means advocate that the Depot should be made to luxurious as to tempt immigrants to stay in it, rather than to betake themselves to the honest toil and struggle which all who are good for anything are prepared to encounter in commencing a new career in a new colony …

The arrangements for cooking appear to be generally sufficient; but the day-rooms and the table and sitting accommodation are certainly not so … Old colonists may be inclined to laugh at the idea of making much of such petty discomforts; but, however much these persons may have uncomplainingly endured and overcome in former times, we do not think that the state of things we have described ought to endure in a Victorian Government institution at the present day.

## Sources

In addition to the newspaper extracts reproduced above, accessed through the National Library of Australia's Trove database (https://trove.nla.gov.au), the author referred to the following:

Haines, Robin F. *Emigration and the Labouring Poor: Australian Recruitment in Britain and Ireland, 1831–60* (Palgrave Macmillan, 1997), pp. 142–65.

Harling, Philip. 'Assisted Emigration and the Moral Dilemmas of the Victorian State', *The Historical Journal*, vol. 59, no. 4 (2016), pp. 1027–1049 [particularly for the *Subraon* scandal].

McClaughlin, Trevor. *Barefoot and Pregnant? Irish Famine orphans in Australia* (2 vols, Genealogical Society of Victoria, 1991–2001).

Moloney Caball, Kay. *The Kerry Girls: Emigration and the Earl Grey Scheme* (The History Press, 2014).

# In Kabul I was Busy Playing

BY MARWA ZAMIR

It is hard to forget them. It was an accident in Kabul, I was busy playing with my sister and my cousin outside my uncle's house when suddenly a horrible sound shocked everything. It was like when you pause a video for a few minutes, then play it back.

The windows were shuttered. I heard people screaming, asking for help. I heard a man yelling so loud, crying *Kumak,* which means *Help* in Farsi. My mum came and said, *Run, go inside.* The kids were crying; they were so scared they were shaking. Even I was. My grandmother made lemon juice for the kids to stop them crying.

Thirty minutes later Mum said, *Let's go home before anything worse happens,* so while walking back the streets were full of policemen, the Afghan force army and American soldiers with big big tanks. I saw dead bodies lying on the street. Mum said, *Just close your eyes, hold my hand and keep walking.*

Two minutes later Mum said we could open our eyes again. We saw a few people cleaning something disgusting like blood, corpses buried in their clothes and burnt iron parts. Women were trying to get closer to the scene of the massacre but the police were not letting them. They kept begging, *Please let me go, my husband is there.* They were crying out so loud that the police let them approach.

I was not crying. I don't know why. I was just staring at the crowd. There was not a single taxi to be found.

Twenty minutes later a taxi appeared. We took it and the taxi driver said, *I will charge you a double fare.* My mum replied, *Just go!* People dead in the streets and the taxi driver was thinking about his business.

We arrived home and my mum started looking for my dad and her own family on the phone. Me and my siblings were sitting waiting on my brother's bed, holding each other's hands and looking at our mother's face. The TV was on for four or five hours. Mum was watching the news and said, *It's late now let's sleep.*

No one slept that night in their room. Every one of us slept with Mum. I was holding my Mum's hand, my sister was holding my mum's feet. Everyone was attached to her. I don't know about the others but I could not sleep. Whenever I closed my eyes I could see the blood and body parts still dressed in their clothes.

I kept my eyes open every minute. I was calling my Mum. That night was too long and frightening. I was counting counting counting every single second in my mind.

# For Marwa

BY CLAIRE HENNESSY

Marwa – when I read your piece I get tears in my eyes.
Not sad. Angry.

Your talent is a flame and I am allegedly here to help it
But honestly all I can do is cheer you on –
Because you are already doing it,
Putting the words together,
Making the magic,
Crafting things that will make a reader breathless,
And you do not need my permission,
Or encouragement,
To do what you do.

But for those flickers of doubt?
Please have it anyway, this permission slip
Because a world where your song goes unheard
Will be lesser.

For whatever it's worth,
Here is the right
To keep being perfectly, beautifully
You.

# Never Again

BY DONATIEN FRANCIS

My name is Donatien Francis and I was born on 19th August 1995 in Bujumbura, Burundi. I am the last born in the family of five children, these are the names of my siblings; Uwimbabazi Brandine, Mushimire Delphine, Uwineza Constance and Emmanuel Rugwiza. Being the last born in the family, my birth was very much unlikely with the fact that my mother delivered all her children in a caesarean section and I was born in the time with the civil war in climax. When my mother gave birth to the third child, the doctors, warned her that it was very unsafe for her to continue giving birth in C-section. Basically they wanted her to stop giving birth but because her first three children were girls and my father was demanding boys my father's relatives started abusing her for not giving births to boys and because she was a pure Tutsi. It came to the point that when my father was away his relatives would come to the house and start insulting, abusing my mother for no reason other than being Tutsi and unable to bear boys. For instance, they would come to her house and go straight to the kitchen, and throw all the food she had cooked on the ground just to show her that she was never liked by my father's family.

Because of the pressure from my father's relatives, my mother ignored the doctor's warning and risked her life and went on to have a fourth child in 1994, luckily it was a boy and a year later I was born.

My father, Francis Sibomana, was born in 1966 and is a Hutu. He was a prominent politician in our region prior to the civil war and was district chairman for the front for Democracy (FRODEBU) for Burundi in the period 1990 to 1997.

He was heavily involved in politics before he fled the county during the civil war in 1997. He was a (FRODEBU) party chairman in the province of Gitega and district of Buraza. My father was a half-caste born from a Tutsi mother and a Hutu father. He has a brother Ngabozinza Festo who was a senior soldier in the army at the time of civil war. He is currently in Rwandan prison since the mid-1990s for crimes arising from the genocide. Being a half-caste my father, together with his brother, was forced to betray either Hutu or Tutsi by killing them. On the other hand, they both fought against Tutsi rebels after the assassination of President Melchior Ndiyaye, which led to civil war.

My father was only six years old when Burundi experienced the first genocide in 1972, my father grew up in hatred environment where a father would kill his own child, a brother would kill his own sister for ethnic reasons. Growing up in this kind of environment my father wanted to be a change he wanted to see and became involved in politics. My father had his brother who also happened to be his best friend. Unlike my father his brother chose to work in the army where he served in the military until the mid-1990s. My father was a very religious and generous man with a good economic status which made him be voted as district chairman for FRODEBU party in his home province Gitega in the early 1990s, the same period when the president of FRODEBU and Burundi was assassinated few months after he was elected.

After years of fighting, like many other families, most of my father's family members were murdered during the civil war and after the subsequent arrest of my uncle, the rebels visited our house in our home village of Gitega, which was close to the Rwandan border. They visited several times looking for my father in order to kill him, together with my siblings. We were only saved because our mother was a pure Tutsi and she was able to protect us from Tutsi militias. Eventually, my father had no choice but to flee the country for his life and for his family including myself as an infant. He fled to Tanzania where he sought asylum and lived in Lumasi refugee camp until it was subsequently closed.

After our father fled Burundi, my mother, Jaqueline Nyirabakarani (born 25th December 1966 and who is a Tutsi), and my siblings escaped from our village of Gitega and we moved to my mother's home village (Cibitoke). We lived there for a couple of months until the civil war was on the climax and the killing had spread in every part of the country.

One night the Hutu militias attacked our village and killed both Tutsi and moderate Hutus. My family was no exception, given that my family was well known in the village and the region, we became an easy target for genocidaires as they knew what ethnic group our family belonged and the political and military roles of my father and uncle. As my mother was a pure Tutsi, almost everyone in her family was butchered. The rebels burnt our house and we fled to the Burundi capital, Bujumbura, where we lived in fear for almost a month. After that, we escaped and sailed through Lake Tanganyika and sought asylum in Tanzania where we were reunited with my father. After a few months in a Tanzanian refugee camp, they're wanted to close the camp. Subsequently, people were subjected to forced repatriation where the Burundian army came into the camp and loaded people into their vehicles while beating them. After things got worse and more unsafe in the camp we managed to leave the camp and went to Malawi where we sought asylum and were given refugee status with the protection of the United Nation High Commission for Refugee (UNHCR) in 2000. This allowed us to reside in Dzaleka Refugee Camp and my family are there now.

Dzaleka was once a maximum security political prison in Malawi, the name Dzaleka is translated as (never again) which means once you have been arrested and taken to Dzaleka prison and if you are lucky to come out alive, you will never commit a crime again.

Unlike Lumasi refugee camp in Tanzania where refugees were living in the tents, in Dzaleka it is almost impossible to live in the tents because of a bad weather in the area and many Malawian locals would not wish to live in that area.

Red Cross, Jesuit refugee service, world food programme, churches and UNHCR are the main non-governmental organizations operating in the camp.

After our arrival in Dzaleka refugee camp when I was five years old in September 2000, we were welcomed by United Nation High Commission for Refugees and taken to its office in the camp for registration. Later we were given a piece of land where we could build our shelter and monthly food for all the family members, which was the 50kg bag of rice and five litres of cooking oil. Some local Malawians surrounding the camp would come into the camp each month end, when there was food distribution and buy some food from refugees who were willing to sell part of their food. This was the only way refugees were able to make money and buy some basic needs like toothbrush, washing soap, tomatoes, onion etc.

This time hundreds of refugees were coming in the camp every day and the camp was expanding each day. I remember our early days in the camp, you could hear hyenas screaming each night and we could find hyena footprints when we wake up in the morning, this was because the camp was more less like a jungle, but with time it all disappeared because more refugees have arrived in the camp and occupied the area.

A month later after we were granted a refugee status which allowed us to continue to reside in the camp up to date, together with my brother we started pre-primary school and my three sisters went to a primary school which were sponsored by UNHCR and Jesuit refugee service (JRS). While in the camp we made friends and met people who we lived with while in Tanzanian camp and in Burundi, we were starting to live a normal life with no war and far from Burundi where Burundian government would not come and repatriate people.

After a year in pre-primary school, my brother and I went to primary school. Because of overcrowding in the camp, there was pressure on resources especially in health and education sector, for instance, you could find a class which was designed to accommodate 40 pupils with over 100 pupils. We stayed in primary for eight years and then got selected to Dzaleka Community Day Secondary School which is located in the camp and run by JRS and UNHCR.

Most people from Rwanda and Burundi in the camp are traumatized and some have mental issues especially those who witnessed their loved ones being murdered. It is no surprise to find people talking and shouting to themselves. I remember one woman from Rwanda who lived few houses away from our house, would wake up early in the morning each day and starts shouting to herself "Kill me as you killed my children". This is the woman who lost all her children including her husband during 1994 genocide in Rwanda.

Because the camp consisted of both Hutu and Tutsi, the same people who were fighting in Burundi, there were incidents where hatred was experienced in the camp, for Hutu would set the Tutsi house on fire, food poison, and it was hard to find Hutu and Tutsi sitting together as friends.

The only hopes in the camp are resettlement and World University of Canada (WUSC) programme but it was never a guarantee that you will be resettled, and it does not matter whether you are a long stay in camp or not, it is just a game of chance. Australia, Finland, Norway, Canada, USA are the main countries which come to the camp and takes out refugees each year. All the people under the age of 24 and have a completed Malawi senior leaving certificate with good grades have a chance to apply for WUSC programme; each year less than 30 students are resettled through this programme.

***

Mosney Accommodation Centre, Atlantic House in Tramore (Waterford) and Birchwood House (Waterford) are three Direct Provision Centre I have lived in Ireland.

Living in direct provision is never easy. I was involuntarily moved from Mosney to Waterford just after September in 2015 and I could not apply for any college or find a course to keep myself busy, it was already too late and I had to wait for another year to try and apply for college. This was the most depressing moment in my life, with no college and living in a very quiet countryside, I could spend the whole day in bed only to wake up to collect food and because we were not allowed to cook, sometimes I could skip meals not because I was not hungry but eating the same meal every day can make someone lose appetite. You can imagine at the age 20 full of energy and hopes, living in a condition where you are not allowed to work and getting €19.10/week - the payment which is not even enough to cover all the necessities which you will need as a human being e.g. body lotion, tooth-brush, phone credit etc. With time I got used to the life in the direct provision but I was constantly thinking about my family in Malawi Refugee camp since I thought when got in Ireland, I will be able to find a job so that I can send some money to my family. I always felt ashamed when I was talking with them on the phone because they knew I came to here with the reason to study, they would tell me not to worry about them and I should just focus on my studies. It could have been very disappointing for them to hear that I was not going to college and, that I was living in direct provision, so sometimes when they "ask about how are my studies", I would just reply to them everything is good but in reality, I was not going to college at all.

I hope one day to finish my studies and get a good job, so that I can be able to help some of my friends I left in the camp and hopefully being a role model to young refugees in Dzaleka refugee camp, because I made my way out of the camp and they can do it too.

## Mentor's Note

BY CHRISTODOULOS MAKRIS

On receiving Donatien Francis' original biographical piece for this project – a brisk, grounded, and at times deeply moving 23-page account of national, family and personal history originating in Burundi and landing in Ireland via refugee camps in Tanzania and Malawi, taking in tribal conflict and civil war, genocide, self-exile and asylum seeking, holding back what would be justifiable anger (which we all indulge in regularly in response to so much less) about the indignities of the direct provision system, and finally full of gratitude and hope in the face of such difficulties rendered matter-of-fact, thus step-by-step revealing a remarkable spirit behind the words – I wondered how we could do it justice within the space afforded to him by the anthology. I felt that if anything the 23 pages were begging to be expanded into a longer, multilayered piece cross-illuminating the conditions Donatien inherited, the complex family history with its collective and individual journeys alongside his personal decisions and objectives. It's clear that we and our policymakers need constant reminders of how easily the unacceptable can become normalised; how utterly commonplace and human the forced migrant experience is and has been throughout history, and how the various comforts any of us are fortunate to enjoy at different times can blind us, often wilfully, to others' everyday and in extreme cases (which sadly abound) brutal circumstances. At first I wanted to avoid a contribution here so that Donatien's writing appears without any sort of mediation – and this is why I proposed to the editors to allow many of the grammatical idiosyncrasies or (from a certain perspective) errors in what ended up being Donatien's own edited account to stand unaltered. But given my insight into so much more than is possible to be represented here at this time, I just wish to place on record this brief note of acknowledgement of his perseverance and spirit. And to underline that experiences like Donatien's, which we must not forget are still evolving in real time, need to be widely documented, amplified, culturally internalised.

# La despedida

by Evgeny Shtorn

*See you soon.* The mere words
bring to my throat
a wave of a hot air.

To approach and say *Aupa* to someone
that I barely know is not a big deal.
Even if this someone looks at you
with too-opened eyes.
Even though this someone
shakes your hand too softly.
Even though.

To maintain a relationship
through messenger and birthday calls,
it's a bit more complicated.
Routine is a very cunning lady.
From time to time she lets me
write for example *'The night is starry…'*,
or a meaningless *How are you?*
Despite bothering me
with burning chicken chest,
or coffee in my old Bialetti,
she lets me write these short sentences
full of typos and misspellings
I know how to deal with her.

Nobody knows
what is awaiting us
just around the corner:
a crazy man with knife,
a civil war,
or a peaceful summer afternoon.
The farewell
suffocates
because we both know
that despite everything there is the probability
we will not meet again.

# They will come for you

BY EVGENY SHTORN

Remember when they come for you
day or more likely night
remember
electric light on the stairs or maybe dark
remember when they come for you
half-finished lemon tea
remember when they come for you
only words smile or silence
when they come for you
when they come for you
they won't remove their leather boots
they won't look at the black and white picture
hanging on the wall
where you are smiling to your aunt
totally happy
ten months old
they will never shrink their heart
when they come for you
remember that mild morning
on the Onega lake
when the water was extremely cold
and extremely inviting
the clearest water you've ever seen
remember that kiss that you give to your best friend
to that tall boy from your school
so good at chemistry
to lose him forever
to keep him forever
in your tired chest
you were woven of these smallest details
when they came for you

## The body of my body

by Evgeny Shtorn

The body slowly disappears
limps and stops
resists and snarls
doesn't want can't doesn't rush
the body disappears slowly
swoons and rests
scars and shows the tongue
not pliable
body harmful
slowly the body disappears
doesn't want
to consult
independent adult body
lonely and rebellious
slowly disappears the body
nothing remains of it
all who accompany the body cry
someone hysterically
someone through laugh
invisible tears
on the black
lipstick
the gap
between the teeth
as a door
to nowhere

# Postscript

by Annemarie Ní Churreáin

*for a country of asylum*

And if, despite borders, you should find yourself
gifted with a new son,
                    you must remember
                              that he owes you
                                        nothing.

He is his own river untangling back and forth from a lamp-lit source.
He is a foster child of the gods.
He is a window opening in search of a country, a mother, a tongue
by which the barely translatable can be spoken.

Your task is simply to hold steady.
Observe in the Oak's shade
the tiniest creatures,
all come-go and busy,
all wise to loss and yet
                    infinitely free in their desires.

Let the *Why? How? What if?* piled up like deadwood fall away.

Even the common Starling, thumbling to the whole world,
knows of roots and earth beyond imagination.

More than curfews, trust
                    the stilly afterlight of a wing.

# Because Justice Matters

BY ANONYMOUS

I gazed into the mirror, and the reflection I saw grabbed all my attention. Though the image looked everything like me, the eyes had no resemblance to mine. Through the eyes I could see a heart filled with sadness, and sorrow. It was at that moment I knew something had gone wrong. As the days passed I questioned myself on what had gone wrong. I couldn't find an answer, but a voice kept whispering:

'Speak out, speak out'.

Each time I went to sleep the voice got louder and louder and louder, till there came a moment when I could no longer remain silent. Was this the voice of power?, I thought. Was this the voice of resurrection?, I imagined. Had I died an emotional and psychological death? It became so unbearable, that I had to do something, I had to speak out. I am speaking out.

I am not speaking out because I am brave, and not because I have the capacity. I am speaking out because I can no longer remain silent. I cannot continue to watch people die emotionally, mentally, and intellectually in the name of protection. I have made a choice. A choice to speak out because justice matters. Lives matter. I matter, they matter, everyone matters. We all matter, and deserve a life of respect and dignity, regardless of status.

Behind my unspoken words is a story, a story of lives trapped behind walls and under ceilings. My story is a hidden one, you cannot see it written on my face as I walk on the streets. It is printed on my heart, written by the ink of my tears, and signed by my emotional scars. To gain a full insight into me as an asylum seeker, why I am here, and how I expect to be supported as I integrate into this new life, all starts from listening. Friends, and fellow countrymen and women, lend me your ears. It is not by choice that I landed here. It is because of the unbearable, inhumane and degrading treatment that I experienced for years in my past life. As a result, I decided to set off on a journey – a journey to 'self-liberation'. Self-liberation that would bring a sense of security and peace. Unknown to many, but known to us the journey is never an easy one, as your destination is unknown and no life is guaranteed. Many have died along the way, many have died in the waters, and many have disappeared without trace.

Having survived all this, upon entering into Ireland I had a great sense of security, as I knew I was now in what they referred to as a safe land, that upholds and vindicates rights for all. Alas, another journey had just begun. A journey of a lifetime, with obstacles requiring endurance. I found myself trapped behind walls, surrounded by fences and far from the outside world. It was at that moment I lost my voice, as I knew that my words couldn't travel. My voice had been trapped behind the walls of protection. I had been separated from the outside world. There were dividing walls on what I could do and enjoy. And this is the place I had to call 'home' now. The moment one arrives at a direct provision centre, one embarks on a second era of unknown struggles. Children are reared trapped behind walls, without a sense of touch to reality. Education, though education is essential to live independently and to gain freedom, is far from reach. The opportunity to become independent and free is quickly cut off at the age of 19 years old. Great skills, great potential, are put to waste. I have come to realise:

I have lost my dignity and sense of being in the name of protection.

When I wake up, like everyone else I see walls but unlike others the walls around me cannot be avoided, they are the order of the day. The environment does not allow me to have the comfort of a home. I feel imprisoned. I am imprisoned. How can I call this place home, when I cannot even have a diet of my own? I wake up to a breakfast that has been carefully chosen by someone else. Do not get me wrong – yes, I am grateful – but it is not something that I would normally eat. How can I call this place home when I have to undress in front of two other people? How can I call this place home when the only room I have for privacy, away from everyone else, has become the bathroom? How can I call this place home, when I cannot have visitors in my own room? How can I call this place home when my own visitors have to sign in and out, in my own place of residency? How can I call this place home when there is a cut off time when I can eat and where I eat from? How can I call this place home when I have a curfew? And how can I call this place home when I am even afraid to speak up? I am not sure anymore whether I am under protection, or whether I am the one others are being protected from. I am watched all the time. I am afraid. I am numb. I am confused. I start to think of home every day, I miss my siblings, I miss the laughter, I miss everyone. I have no one here I can relate to, and no one who can relate to me. I am on my own.

One Thursday morning, as usual I went to collect my €19 from the main post office. Unknown to me this was no usual Thursday morning. I entered the direct provision bus, and as usual there was a lot of silence. No one was talking, all I could hear was the innocent babies crying. I guessed everyone was busy thinking of their struggles and when the struggles would end. I felt like I had no confidence.

Perhaps, I thought, when I got out of the bus I would meet different people with a different mind-set, who might uplift my day. Alas! My confidence was knocked down even more. As I walked down the street, heading towards the shopping mall after collecting my €19, I heard monkey-like screams straight in my ear. As I turned back I was told:

'Go back to the jungle.'

What did he mean? Was this really necessary? Was it really worth saying? Worth shouting at me? I did not expect to hear words like this in the 21st century. From that day I lost confidence in people, in myself, in society and the world at large. Being exposed to such words, created an additional daily stressor for me. On this day I came to learn that:

Skin colour plays a large part in how people are viewed, valued and treated.

After this, I became very worried about my future. I was constantly worried about my tomorrow. Little did I know that this, combined with the direct provision centre pressures, was going to affect my psychological and physiological health in the future. But I did know one thing: I now knew I was alone. I went back to the place I called home in tears; my heart was bleeding heavily. 'I guess,' I thought, 'this is where I belong'.

Since I have to spend more time there than anywhere else, I try my best to make myself at home, but I struggle. It is unbearable. I witness families forced to live in single rooms. I witness residents with mental difficulties left unaddressed and unattended to and forced to adapt to the same standards as everyone else. I witness people self-harming as they cannot bear the pain of returning home after spending countless years in the centres, people who have lost half of their lifetime. I witness children taking turns to play with just one toy. I witness people fighting over using washing machines and dryers. I witness vulnerable women exchanging their bodies for money. Every day I witness terror. I cry. Was this a wall of protection or was it a separator, and a divider?

Terror cannot vanish easily. It does not simply go away. This is why, after the journey, I had to pour out my heart. Hoping that my past and fears will be buried behind. Hoping that this piece will bring hope to the many lost lives. Hoping that policy makers will gain an insight into life in direct provision and join the call on ending direct provision. Though not easy, I am also hoping that my fellow countrymen and women acknowledge the presence of diversity and embrace multiculturalism. The experience in direct provision centre is a rambling and overwhelming one. We strive for nothing other than liberation, recognition and a peace of mind, but it is so far from our reach. Hear me and hear us:

*No one leaves home unless home is the mouth of a shark.*

## Repeating the Mistakes of the Past

BY EMILIE PINE

For most of the 20th century, Ireland had a system of residential institutions for children and women, run by the Catholic Church and funded and overseen by the Irish State. These institutions – known as Industrial Schools, Magdalene Laundries, and Mother and Baby Homes – incarcerated vulnerable members of the population, justifying these actions through a discourse of 'care'. In reality, the children and women forced to live in these institutions suffered systemic abuse, including physical, emotional and sexual abuse.

We might ask how could a system of containment, in which abuse was perpetrated, be maintained for so many decades? Sadly, the answer is not because no one knew, but because people knew but did not intervene.

There are social and cultural explanations – the dominance of the Catholic Church made it very difficult for survivors and their supporters to speak out. As one survivor put it, 'They were gods, who would question them?' Indeed, abuse survivors who were able to talk about what had happened to them, were often not believed or, if believed, told to be quiet. For the most part, these were the children and sisters and mothers of the poor. Poverty counted against them, in the first place leading to their institutionalisation, and in the second undermining the social value of their testimony. As a result, once released from an institution, many people emigrated to escape the stigma and shame that a narrow-minded, hierarchical and insular society labelled them with. They were Ireland's scapegoats.

Since the 1990s, that shame began to shift, from the victim to the perpetrators. As more survivors found audiences for their stories, the public began to understand, and to admit, the hurt that had been done. In 1999, Taoiseach Bertie Ahern apologised to the survivors of childhood abuse, 'on behalf of the state and all its citizens … for our collective failure to intervene, to detect their pain, to come to their rescue.' Following this long overdue admission of culpability, the state funded the Commission to Inquire into Child Abuse. The publication in 2009 of the CICA Report (known as the Ryan Report) proved conclusively that abuse had been systemic in the Industrial Schools. Though a flawed document, this Report caused a major social change in societal attitudes, leading to widespread support for survivors' rights. Following in the wake of the Ryan Report, both the McAleese Report on Magdalene Laundries (2013) and the currently ongoing Mother & Baby Homes Commission, demonstrate that the history of *all* of Ireland's institutions needs to be investigated, owned up to, and compensated for.

We now know, based on the stories of survivors, and the thousands of pages of official reports, that, at best, large institutions are dehumanising. At worst, however, they are marked by a pervasive culture of abuse. Institutions are not an adequate response to the question of how to shelter and care for a vulnerable group of people.

It is more than ten years since the publication of the Ryan Report and it would be nice to think that not only is Ireland's institutional history well and truly over, but society and the state have learned the lessons of the past.

But it seems we have not. We still lock a lot of very vulnerable people away. We are doing it every day, and we are ignoring it every day. And this is not just how emotional and physical and sexual happens, this is an abuse in itself.

The system of Direct Provision Centres repeats the mistakes of the past. As a system it shows that Ireland is not wiser or more careful or more compassionate than it was in the 1950s. Instead, we are still capable of gross structural callousness, still capable of withholding the basic respect due to our fellow humans, and still capable of closing our minds to the abuse happening right in front of us.

## Visual art

by Hina Khan

# Philodendron

by Stephen Sexton

Hardly the narrow lanes of Kopardal,
not much more than bridleways
made avenues on either side
by verdure and prettiness;
blue spruces, saxifrage, astrantia,
fields of Scandinavian grasses,
sweeping south towards the coast
where the ferry idles in the port.

Not that village, and no ideal,
but the flat-packed bed-frame
machined from powder-coated steel
and laid out in a loose orchestration
of perimeter, rope-ladder slats,
schema, screws and Allen keys;
the little bag of latent torque
in its chaperone of plastic.

Were now centuries ago,
from the little porthole of a hulk
or some meandering prison ship,
I might have been seen at the same work
in the olfact of an oak grove;
to genuflect and curse some rude sapling
or cord or length of timber
which will not be managed into shape.

We might sleep tonight on quilts
of jewel flower or philodendron,
while in estuaries and anchorages
fleets of prison ships amass and moor
and the sun slips beyond the wave,
or we might long from the portholes
and pray to those asleep on quilts
of jewel flower or philodendron.

# Songs of Innocence, Songs of Experience

BY BATUR NADIR

1. The Past is not a Distant Place (Prior to leaving Kabul)

For the past two weeks in Kabul, rival forces pounded each other. Then came a short ceasefire that provided an opportunity for escape. It was a scorching summer's day. I saw a lot of people fleeing, wounded children being carted in wheelbarrows. People piggybacking their essential belongings such as rags, mattresses, cooking pots.

Children were screaming and the elderly recited verses from the Koran. They all wanted to get out of Kote Sangi. On the way, I saw a lot of dead bodies and corpses that were swollen and smelled of a million dead and rotting rats. Exiting the dusty alleys of our neighbourhood, we entered Kote Sangi Chowk roundabout, where smells of gunpowder were still fresh. Entire blocks of shops and schools were turned into rubble.

I heard heavy firing followed by rocket explosions. I saw men and women falling in the street. I saw a man dropping his disabled grandmother from his back to escape shooting.

We were the lucky ones who made it safely to Kompany area, where we paid a tall, dust-stained, bearded lorry driver to get us to Maidan Shar, Kharote village where we were to stay in my maternal uncle's house 'till the war was over in Kabul.

The road was dusty and very bumpy. The faster the car travelled, the more dust and jolting we received. Scorched by the sun and choked with dust, we finally arrived. Scars and wounds from the Soviet war were still visible. Bombed out ruined houses, rusty corpses of Russian tanks were lying in their final graveyards.

2. Dublin (First Direct Provision Hostel)

As an asylum seeker, I was not allowed to work, could not avail of training facilities, not allowed to cook, and faced restrictions in relation to visitors and travel. I was given €19.10 a week and three meals a day while awaiting the decision of my asylum application. I was accommodated in a short-stay hostel with the impending intention of relocation to another hostel outside of Dublin.

The hostel was an old building; white plaster crumbled off its walls. But I thought I was living in a mansion. I had food in my belly, a roof over my head and I had no fear of rocket fall. What else could an Afghani man fleeing from hell ask for in life? After a short stay I was transferred to Carlow.

3. Carlow

I didn't know much about Carlow. The next morning, four of us refugees (two Somali and one Sudani) were loaded onto a bus like a herd of sheep. I slept on the bus, not having had any sleep the night before. I woke to the driver voice shouting 'Wake up, we have arrived'.

Construction work had temporarily blocked the entrance so the bus driver parked the bus in station, and we walked to the hostel. Rain had just ceased but water was still falling from the branches of trees. Clouds were dispersing and the wet earth emitted a pleasant after-rain odour. Across from the station a bunch of robins were occupying a willow tree. They were screaming and quarrelling. It is said that robins – like humans – have aggressive territorial behaviour.

We waddled behind the bus driver like baby elephants following their mother. The bus driver held a black umbrella in his right hand like a tourist guide. As we were walking through Carlow Town Centre, one of the Somali lads with a long neck became tired of carrying his bag of clothes by one hand. So, he placed the bag on his head. I smiled to myself. It reminded me of the village in Afghanistan, when mother and other ladies carried pots, buckets and baskets in this way. Much to my surprise, he abruptly unloaded the bag from his head when one of his countrymen gave him an angry look and told him something in Somalian language. Perhaps he told him it was not suitable behaviour for this country.

4. Allowance

Over the next few months, I settled in the Milverton House, met many people and became familiar with rules and regulations. One morning, I rose too late. The clock on the blue painted wall showed me half nine.

Downstairs, the kitchen stank of chlorine bleach mingled with the rancid smell of oil. Breakfast was finished. I implored for a drink of orange, but was not given it. I had to wait until lunch to eat. My €19 weekly entitlement had been spent on buying a Mach 3 razor, and a lottery ticket; hoping I would become a millionaire. Out of the remaining two euros I had bought a bottle of seven up as I had a tummy bug.

The man who refused me the orange drink was abusive, 'Are you stupid or what! Don't you see my hands are busy.'

Later, in the anteroom, I sat on a red sofa (that had several cigarettes burns) in a pensive mood. My feeling of indignation rose not from the denial of orange juice but from the offensive words. After all, the man who said them had been an asylum seeker like me a few years before.

5. Charity Shop

'You have to fucking go to bed early to get up early bud,' Mark, a kitchen orderly said.

'I can't sleep early,' I replied.

'Every day you're sitting on your ass on this sofa, dandling this fucking remote control. Find work or do something to make you tired,' Mark ordered.

'I am not allowed to work. How can I work?' I nearly shouted in response.

'Would you do some volunteer work in a charity shop?'

'Yes,' I replied. My heart was lighter that night at the prospect of having something to do.

Next morning, light rain had splattered the earth, and weather was still cloudy. When Mark and I reached the charity shop, a woman in her mid-thirties was smoking outside the shop.

'Howya . Joanne, I have an Afghani volunteer for you,' Mark said.

An expression of alarm spread across Joanne's face. Inside the shop, I sniffed damp odour from old clothes.

Alison, in her late twenties, was sorting bric-a-brac behind the counter. The moment I entered the shop, an uncanny feeling told me that Joanne and Alison disliked me. One day, when I was sorting clothes, I eavesdropped them talking about me.

'How is the foreign lad?' Alison asked.

'He seems nice, but kind of weird,' Joanne replied.

'Yeah, they are all nicey, nicey. Let him get his passport, he will wipe the country,' Alison whispered.

6. Application Refused

After two years in Carlow, my application was returned, denied. The door to the future seemed closed that day. I was facing deportation back to Afghanistan. The letter inside that brown envelope tore me to pieces. Gloomier still, the hostel in Carlow was closing. Residents were to be relocated to New Ross, County Wexford.

7. En Route to New Ross

Summer has gone and winter was in its place. It is chilly and foggy day; light flakes of snow are descending further melancholy to the scene. About twenty of us are waiting for the bus. Everyone is wearing heavy clothing, holding bags that contain total sum of their personal belonging. Some seem happy, some seem moody, some are chatty, some are reflecting, some are puffing on cigarettes, and some are puffing out warm air onto their hands.

Miles passed with no houses and then, in the centre of nowhere, at the bottom of a hill, a house appeared with smoke flying from its chimney and a bulb shining in its kitchen. I imagine in each house people living with their parents, brothers, sisters, relatives, smiling, gossiping, chatting with no worries about deportation or relocation. This thought makes me envious, and I lament the hierarchy of human life. Some people spend their entire life in pain, owing to misfortunes of birth in the wrong place; they are considered stupid, poor, uncivilised and outcast from the society.

These thoughts passed through me, then disappear, when my gaze falls on a row of trees standing on a stretch of road near New Ross, extending their limbs from either side to form a canopy.

8. New Ross

The 'Old Rectory' hostel is located on high ground opposite the River Barrow. Living standards here were a lot higher than my previous two locations. Rooms were clean; two to three people shared a single room. The dining hall was spacious and the anteroom had a snooker table. At this stage I was a grown man of 28 years but inside felt like a child. My days were riddled with anxieties and nights were haunted by nightmares of Ali. That childhood trauma never left me; it often resurfaced during dark hours to suffocate me further, to drag me into more blackness.

9. Infidels Make Everything (The Spoils of War)

Kids in the village of New Ross were a lot different than kids in Kabul: there, they moseyed around bare footed, grazed sheep, fetched water, collected dung and played marbles all day long. They had rough skin, chapped hands and feet.

It often intrigued me to see an egg left on top of one of the children's graves. Later, I found out that the child had kept an egg in his hand when his dead body was dug out from under the rubble of a bombed-out bunker. As a mark of respect to the child's memory, people often put an egg on his grave.

As a young boy, I was drawn to one particular kid, named Younis. He was well mannered, lanky with a brown complexion, almond shaped nomadic blue eyes, bushy eyebrows and a wide, flat nose. He was about twelve.

Around that time, Pakistani merchants were coming to the village to buy shrapnel, fragments of destroyed tanks, shells or other objects thrown out by explosions. They paid one thousand Afghani in exchange for one kilogram of shrapnel which would then be exported to Pakistan for melting and casting into new iron.

This business of collecting and selling was a source of income. To think of it now makes my stomach cringe. Russian scientists made booby trap bombs to resemble toys to get Afghani children to pick them up. Those toys had wounded and killed many children. Leaving them with and hands and feet blown away.

The irony is that those toy bombs were a direct copy of an American device used in Vietnam, the BLU-43B. I sometimes wonder how on earth civilised men, in white hats, enlightened by science and reason, can ever think that children are part of their war.

One morning, at sunrise, me and Younis embarked on a quest to collect shrapnel. We were soaked in sweat by the time we reached the tallest peak of the Sangimarmar mountain. The sun was glazing and sweat was trickling down our faces. By lunch we had gathered enough shrapnel to fill two rubber buckets. I accidently encountered two piles of debris which were large missiles half sunk into the ground. 'Look here, two big ones!' I shouted to Younis.

'Too heavy,' he whispered but after a moment of reflection, he said, 'Let's cut bushes to put on top of these metals.'

'But why?' I asked, a little bewildered.

'If anyone sees these, they will bring shovels and dig them out,' Younis replied.

'But they are too heavy to be taken down to the village,' I countered.

Younis narrowed his eyes. 'They can be rolled down from the mountain, you softy Kabuli'.

We became very tired after hours of roving over those mountains. We sat under the shadow of a big stone and stretched our legs. I was finding great relief whenever the cool mountain breeze was touching my face but was feeling extremely hungry. Younis took out a piece of bread from his pocket, sliced it into two pieces and gave one to me.

A few meters away, my gaze fell on a rusty battery. 'Look, there is another toy bomb,' I said.

Younis went close, picked it 'No, this is not a bomb, it's a battery. Mujahideen use it in Mokhabera'.

'Mokhabera, what is this?' I asked.

'It is something that Mujahideen use to talk to each other from the distance without seeing each other.' Younis had an attitude of pride in his tone.

A feeling of inferiority rose inside me. To boost my fragile ego, I began to show off my shrewdness.

'Do you know electricity? We had electricity in Kabul.'

'No, I have never heard of it, never seen it,' Younis replied.

'You go and press a button on the wall. This brings light under the ceiling, which is a lot brighter than the light in a lantern,' I said.

10. Friends

I had been living in Ireland for three years well integrated into Irish society. I made friends. I always felt a sense of kinship with Irish people. Maybe due to the shared histories between the country of my birth, Afghanistan and my newly adopted country, both moulded in the despair of war, oppression and immigration.

# Workhouse

BY EILEEN CASEY

Perched on the outskirts of town, hidden from prying eyes.
Blind windows, boarded over, the roof fallen in.
Layers of bramble fences. *Keep out* and
*Trespassers Beware* signposted. Were it habitable,
a perfect setting to house Asylum Seekers.

Scant evidence remain of Orphan Girls who left
in famine times on an open Bianconi coach. Crossed
from Cobh to Plymouth, boarded ships for Australia.
A journey of six months tossed on treacherous seas,
heart-sore. Once ashore, they were given shelter,
weekly rations. Tea, sugar, flour.
Direct Provision by another name.

Swallows migrate from the workhouse, return to nest
high in the eaves each spring. Flit between familiar
joists. Unlike the Orphan Girls who never made it
home. Every summer, curls of wild berries glut
hedgerows in the lanes around the workhouse.

Asylum Seekers are also chapters to be written. Stories
of their coming and their leaving. Why the myriad fruits
they brought went un-picked. All that ripeness spilled
into sullen earth. Yet another harvest spent.

# Borders

BY INSAF YALCINKAYA

Look!
People draw borders
Some, in their own lands
Some, in the mind and heart
Like a death circle of Ezidi
Beware! Don't draw the circle.
You are doomed inside,
With me outside

I was born there,
I don't have to die there.

Look!
This is war
This is death
This is poverty
This is hunger
Everywhere artifice
Behind every individual cruelty

Everyone suffocates in their own tragedy
Like drowning in a spoon of water.

Look!
I drown in the seas
That is not my body
People's selfishness washes ashore.
I die due to your borders
I drown due to lovelessness and loneliness.

I'm waiting at the border, the limit - of your imagination
Your heart beats in the left
But does it beat correctly and conscientiously?

I'm waiting at your borders
You ask 'Do you know my language?'

Do I care
How many languages you know?
Where is your humanity?
How is your heart language?

I'm looking for a flame
In your eyes
In your soul.
It seems,
Prometheus never put in an appearance in your lands.

Hatred in your eyes.
Ice covering your heart
Your voice - cold and perishing.

Let me break the ice in your heart.
My bosom as burning as Amaterasu's fire.

Let me become your breath
with primeval words of Humanity

Let me look through your eyes
Let me flow through your eyes into your heart
with deathlessness and depth of legendary loves.

The storm gathers,
My foundations are shattered.
Can you repair the destruction of my soul?
Because of them, because of you.

Look!
Endless middle-eastern war in my soul
Touch me.

Kiss my heart that bleeds
Let me smell your scent,
No longer smell the blood.

Kiss my orphan lips
Embrace the feelings
Accumulating at your border

I'm waiting at the door of your heart
With my asylum seeker soul
Open your heart
Let me in.

*Ezidi: an ethnic group of Kurds dispersed and persecuted in Syria, Turkey, Iran and Iraq (Kurdistan)*
*Amaterasu: a goddess in Japanese Mythology*

# A Worthless Life?

BY INSAF YALCINKAYA

Around a table
We strike a bargain for my life
They think
I'm just a number
My life is worthless

I put my knowledge up for sale
My art, my poems, my music
They are not interested in them
They are worthless

I put my happiness up for sale
They don't want happy people
Happiness is worthless

I put my hopes up for sale
My future, my dreams
Their border is priceless
My hopes are worthless

I put my sorrows up for sale
my tears, my deep griefs
They want to buy them
to pretend they are merciful
They should take pity on me
Their mercy is priceless
But my humanity is worthless

What a stupid bargain for a worthless life
Meaningless words between their lips.
What a stupid life.
All its riches – worthless.

# Are You Proud?

BY INSAF YALCINKAYA

1

My city, Dersim,
crushed with a bronze fist,
is in danger.
My people, how can you praise
someone who laughs in your face?
Who forces you to listen
to the blaring of Ezan
from sun to sun?
Your Pirs set a table for bastard men.
Our Pirs would not let their dogs behave like you.

2

Are you proud of your children's high career?
The most noble profession is teaching
but they are taught to represent a fascist system.
A new generation has forgotten
honour, sharing, how to offer
a real contribution-in the name of assimilation.

3

At the back of beyond a poet is executed
On the other side a troubadour is excoriated
A writer is shot in the back
A youth commits suicide
A child is murdered by rape under the blue sky
A child is married off in order to legalized her rape
A woman and yet another woman and one more woman is killed
For want of value in the holy books

Are you still proud of yourself
for being a racist in your leisure time:
you represent a rancid system.

Are you still proud of yourself
in spite of all these things
when you look in a mirror
are you really proud of yourself?

*Pir: Spiritual leader of the Alevi community. This is an inherited role, passing through generations of men and women.*

# The Arrival of Shahmaran – with Apologies to St Patrick

BY KATIE DONOVAN

*for Insaf, Dun Laoghaire, May 2019*

Wafts of bergamot
warming our fingers,
we share tea,
and stroll by the water.
I've been cradled here,
among layers of blue
and snuffling seals.

Suffused with memories
of your lost coast,
you offer snapshots:
feasts of fish and refreshing wine,
bare arms in balmy heat,
old loves; old persecutions.

And Shahmaran:
serpentine goddess
of the city of Mardin,
beloved of Kurds,
wise keeper of a fertile garden.

I am ashamed –
my birthplace blighted
by Medusa fears,
its garden withers,
crammed with the bones
of the banished.

Oh Shahmaran:
I offer you our best tradition
of one thousand welcomes;
we need you here.

# Pain

BY NNGCOBO BONGAMAHLUB

I am a woman and I weep
I weep for a whole nation
I weep for the child who never lived
who never had the chance to breathe
the blossom air or the sweetness of flowers in bloom

the child who was never been kissed by the sun's warmth
or felt the way rain drops on baby skin.

Yes, I weep

I weep for these children born to war
born to famine

I weep for the child born to struggle
whose mother wakes at dawn
and falls asleep late into dark night
searching out ways to feed a family.

Yes, I weep

I weep for the child who is born today.

Who will guide my child?
Where is Ubuntu|Humanity?

Yes - I am scarred and in pain
Yes - I bleed from deep places
blood spills over
weeping
but I am strong
I am a strong woman
I will fight for the future
For the future of my children.

South Africa
will be strong again
though
through barbed wires
I struggle.

I have lost my children
the scars are deep, unhealing.

# At First Glance

BY NNGCOBO BONGAMAHLUB

I'm speechless
but I can see beauty.

Someone with a hidden truth,
a hidden pride.

I wanna be her, have some peace,
calm = ubuntu | botho

I see light wherever she goes,
her beads represent my life, my truths.

Some will think that I wear them to show off,
but they free me,
help me understand the path I am trying to travel,
for someone to ask, on my journey,
who are you?

Yes my beads got meaning
I say with confidence

I am not afraid to be my ancestors,
to embrace my culture,
to embrace what's mine.

I am here...I have arrived,
I am a child of this world
I am a child of Idlozi | Ancestors
I will celebrate this,
in my own way.

# Somewhere, Someone Else

by Elaine Feeney

At the MacDonald's in
Oświęcim
someone has ordered a fillet-o-fish and
two Happy Meals
& decides to wait outside near the square in the
day's summer heat until their number's called.

In a Kazimierz café
the waiter recommends me the white
from Alsace

& because today is unanswerable (& unbearable) - I order the bottle.

Was there ever a moment where
nothing was spoken for no one had song?

I drink the wine.

I am at it again, despite all warnings - spiraling.

Somewhere, someone in France grew these grapes & then crushed them &
someone else's hands held green glass melting, blew it, until it took this hardened
shape
I throttle by the neck.

Somewhere, someone else's print is carved to this walnut chair I sit on.

We are never fully truly alone.

Somewhere, someone has hurled a mattress from a high rise
window as someone extinguishes a fire

& somewhere else, hands stitch a rainbow flag together, while somewhere,
someone other glues black & white lines on a red cloth spread across a kitchen
table
& later goosesteps to *close our borders*

as though a border is an unused shop shutter
as though a border exists only on paper, is redrawn only on paper
as though a border can be kept | owned | like a dog | tied up

here is my tree – here is my stream – here is my air & here is the moon,
*my moon, for somewhere, someone landed there with my flag*

somewhere, someone has choked a woman closed &
someone else is stumbling from a Chinese dinghy upon warm sand without their child

while somewhere, someone else has fallen from the sky into a
London garden.

Somewhere, sometime, someone else has been made to sit a while,
& wait.

# 905976-14

BY DONNAH VUMA

905976-14, the number that identifies me and my three children for the five years that we have been resident in Ireland. From the moment we landed in Dublin and declared that we are seeking international protection, all documents that identify us as individuals where taken away from us and replaced with a blue ID card. This card bears an identification number and states in bold red letters that it is not an identity card. I knew from that moment that we had become a statistic, another bed number!

Seeking asylum is not a crime, it is a fundamental human right that should be safeguarded by all nations. Ireland is a signatory to the Geneva Convention and is therefore obligated to uphold that right. It is extremely unfortunate that seeking protection and safety comes at the price of one's freedom. Direct provision as a system does not allow you to heal, to forget and to move on with your life. It is impossible to go through the day without reliving your past traumas. You live in constant fear of being called into interview and having forgotten any detail about when and where a particular incident occurred. Should you forget, you are deemed to be inconsistent and fabricating your fear therefore meaning that your claim for protection is bogus.

The international protection system and direct provision system in Ireland are both extremely cruel, discriminatory, racist and violate the most basic human rights. It is a profit-making system that thrives on the misery of vulnerable human beings, it is a system that benefits private contractors multi millions every year. As an asylum seeker in Ireland, you are forced to live in limbo and in forced poverty due to state-imposed limitations and discrimination with no rights to basics such as the right to work and the right to education.

When people leave their home countries to seek asylum, driven out by unbearable situation that pose a danger to their lives, though they leave behind most of their materialistic possessions, there are certain things that one cannot and does not leave behind, things such as education, skills, expertise, dreams and ambitions for themselves and their children. People flee with the hope to be able to start or continue living a meaningful life as with any individual in a 'normal' situation. We are forced to live in isolated centers that are segregated from local communities, we are forced to raise families on a meagre income of €38.80 a week.

In 2018 Ireland opted into the EU directive that brought Ireland in line with many EU member States but evidently did very little to provide a meaningful right to work for International Protection applicants. When Ireland opted into the EU Directive on Reception Conditions, the Department of Justice said that some

3000 people would qualify for the permit which the department considers to be generous. But only 330 people have actually secured work with the new permit out of 1521 permits issued to people living in direct provision.

The difficulty with the permit is that it is granted on a piece of paper when other non-EU/EEA workers in Ireland have a GNIB or Irish Residency Permit Card. As such, many employers do not know much about it and applicants have to explain it themselves to potential employers. The second problem with it is that the permit is valid for six months and is renewable. But the uncertainty over renewal and it being valid for six months already limits employment to short-term, usually low paying contacts. Then once a person has been working for at least 12 weeks, they must pay to live in direct provision or find alternative accommodation. It is already difficult enough for people who have been granted protection to leave direct provision with some taking between 6-18 months to find accommodation. So, the prospect of paying to live in direct provision is very real.

The other major problem with the permit is that it's only issued to people who have been waiting for a first instance decision for at least 9 months. It means for 9 months a person will not be allowed to work. And those who have been in the system longer, mainly in the appeals stage of the application process, are disqualified from working which increases the pool of people who are working in slave-like conditions for as little as €50 per week because they are desperate to provide for their needs. If €50 per week means avoiding having to ask a contractor appointed by the government for a slice of bread or cup of coffee, then it is worth it for many people in the system. Unfortunately, restrictions on work rights has normalised these conditions.

We cannot talk about direct provision and its violation of human rights without addressing the violations of the rights of the Child. This is an issue of major concern. The 2000+ children living in direct provision are not entitled to any social welfare benefits including the Child benefit allowance which is given to Irish national children and children of Non-EU citizens legally working in the state. Children have the right to a loving and nurturing environment; direct provision is not a loving and nurturing environment. On the contrary, it is often a hostile space that must be shared with strangers, it is a space where children are exposed to inappropriate behaviors, nudity, language and conversations. There is no space for physical play or mental stimulation required by a developing child. Children are forced to follow a monotonous routine, everything is done the exact way it was done the day before.

All children have the right to health care and nutrition, but children living in direct provision go for years without knowing the taste of their own mother's cooking. The centers often don't have self-catering facilities, meals are on a two-day rotation menu served at specific times three times a day. There is no special menu for children to ensure that the dietary needs of a developing child are met or to ensure that the food is specifically prepared for their young palates, and this often leads to many health problems. Those children must go to school and interact with many children whose parents are able to provide for their needs. Children in direct provision have their school lunches prepared by a contactor that is appointed by the government. The contactor decides what their school lunch will be.

There are other simple things that children do to have a childhood worth remembering like going on holiday with the family or going out to the movies with friends from school. Teens in direct provision are robbed of ordinary teen experiences of life and have the added stress of knowing that no matter how well they do in school, they may not access third level education if they are not lucky enough to get a scholarship. Children have the right to equal opportunity and quality education; this is not a reality for children living in direct provision. The government introduced a higher education pilot support scheme, part of the qualifying criteria is that students completing leaving cert (secondary school) looking to progress onto higher or post leaving cert courses, should have been a minimum of five years in the Irish education system as of 31 August 2017, and have been an applicant for protection or leave to remain for a combined period of five years, and not pending a deportation order. If a deportation order has been issued that child is automatically disqualified from availing of the scheme.

The obvious impact of not being allowed to work, access further education and living in limbo with the threat of deportation and everything that comes with direct provision, is huge on the mental health of a person. You can see the effects manifest in many ways; drug and alcohol addiction, gambling addiction and the recent increase in suicide and suicide attempts. People who are in the asylum process had jobs in their countries and suddenly they are not able to work and provide for their needs and for their loved ones. These are people who have already lost so much of what it means to live a normal life in their countries then their chosen place of sanctuary robs them of that ability to provide for themselves. Both parents and children in direct provision experience mental health problems because of the State sanctioned poverty they live in.

The restrictions on working rights and education rights create communities from asylum and refugee background that have difficulty entering the labour market once they are eventually granted some form of protection. Most people would have spent a long time without a real right to work and thus have a huge gap in the CVs. And other barriers like language, foreign qualifications and discrimination against Africans in the workplace contribute to the difficulty of integration of people with asylum background. People who were once able to provide for their needs are suddenly stripped of that right and must depend on the State's cruel system of direct provision. Getting a simple slice of bread or trip to the dentist to clean teeth becomes a Herculean task all because the government has decided that asylum seekers must live in poverty while their applications are pending.

We need to realize children are like sponges, they watch and absorb everything we do as adults, things we pay attention to and those that we don't. The situation created by the direct provision system is troubling and dangerous. We are raising the future residents of Irish society in a place that is teaching them that it is acceptable to be dependent and helpless and that it is acceptable to be able to live on charitable handouts way below the poverty line. We are showing our children that a living allowance increase from €19.10 to €38.80 is something worth celebrating. Can you then imagine what happens when you move that individual from €38.80 to a week to €180 per week?

Institutionalizing and warehousing human beings is unacceptable and mother to a list of endless problems. Nobody should ever be placed in a situation where they feel like they are less than human. Seeking asylum is not a crime, it is a human right that we are all entitled to. It is unacceptable and unforgivable that children are being forced to grow up in these conditions. The system of direct provision needs to be abolished immediately. No one should ever be allowed to benefit financially from the vulnerability of other people.

#enddirectprovision
#onechildisonechildtoomany

# An Inessential Journey

BY ARNOLD THOMAS FANNING

*Mentoring a writer who lives at a far remove from oneself involves a choice: communicate over that distance remotely or meet after travelling.*

*The writer I am mentoring, Donnah Sibanda Vuma, is originally from Zimbabwe, and currently lives in the Direct Provision System in Knockalisheen Accommodation Centre in Co. Clare, while I live in a rented converted artisan cottage in Midleton, Co. Cork. I decide a face-to-face meeting to discuss her writing project will be more beneficial to her than communicating over the phone or other means. Further, I foresee an opportunity to interview her more personably about her circumstances and her journey from Zimbabwe to Ireland: how she came to be here, in her own words. I will also ask her if I can go and see the Direct Provision Centre she lives in, to be witness as to what that could be like.*

*My plan, as I initially envisage it, is to travel by coach to Limerick Bus Station and then on by local bus to Knockalisheen Accommodation Centre's visitor reception so as to conduct our mentoring meeting and interview, and to see the Centre.*

*Accordingly, I plan to travel.*

The journey to Knockalisheen Accommodation Centre, my journey, begins in my mind, I am little more than a "mental or stationary traveller."[1] I map and plan my route and timetable, my full itinerary and travel plans, in detail, far in advance of the meeting. I know where I am going, and how. I know the cost, physical, emotional, mental, economic.

I do not need to worry, I will go, I will return, safe in the knowledge that I am comfortably able to do so, and I will later recount what I have seen as story, as writing[2], the story of a journey.

A journey is travel, is an excursion, is wandering, is a migration, a passage, a quest, an odyssey. Is egress, is ingress[3].

What drives me to make this journey, which after all, is optional, a journey I have chosen to make? What are my motives? There is a professional impetus, to do full justice to my role as mentor to the best of my ability, and I do feel this is best executed in person. But there is also, undeniably, curiosity; for I do wish to see, for myself, a Direct Provision Centre, be witness to one, and record one in words, as an outsider, for the veracity of this account.

---

1 Merlin Coverly, *Psychogeography*, Herts, 2010, p21.

2 Ibid.

3 *Collins English Dictionary*, Glasgow, 1995.

This makes me plan the trip to include the final leg, from Limerick Bus Station, to Knockalisheen Accommodation Centre, accordingly.

What drives the Asylum Seeker to travel?

"Arbitrary arrests and detentions… economic instability, drought, and unemployment… crack down[s] on dissenting voices… forced evictions… the military… the police… restricted rights[s] to freedom of expression… failure to implement reforms… extreme poverty… a crisis in healthcare service delivery… unavailability of water… shortages of essential medicines and equipment."[4]

The Asylum Seeker's journey is an essential one. My journey is an elective one, made, I am becoming increasingly conscious, on a whim.

The mode of transport I intend to take to Knockalisheen Accommodation Centre is the 303 bus from Limerick City Centre, which involves about half an hour's walking in addition to its journey time of twenty minutes, and starts at 7.35AM, ending at 11PM. The RIA report on Knockalisheen Accommodation Centre's travel arrangements for residents indicates that there is a bus provided from the Centre to Limerick City Centre three times a day, starting at 10AM and finishing at 5.15PM[5]. Because the Asylum Seeker's income is heavily restricted, many are limited to the DPC's transport service, as the cost is otherwise prohibitive. I, without such limitations, have therefore more choice: for travel, for egress, for ingress.

Research indicates that there is no official database that details statistics on modes of transport or methods of travel for Asylum Seekers[6]. But anecdotal evidence suggests that Asylum Seekers have travelled by a plethora of methods to arrive at the ultimate destination of their journeys: by car, by boat, by plane, by bus, by train, by lorry, and on foot[7].

I have chosen to travel by public transport: by local bus to Cork City, and then by Expressway bus from Cork to Limerick Bus Station, then on by local bus again to Knockalisheen Accommodation Centre.

But the fact is that I have the option to drive, in my own car, if I want.

---

4 *Amnesty International Report 2017/18*, 'Zimbabwe', pp405.

5 *Reception and Integration Agency Report for Knockalisheen Accommodation Centre 18.11.17*, Section 14, 'Transport Arrangements'.

6 Irish Refugee Council, personal correspondence.

7 *The Irish Times*, 'New to the Parish', various dates.

Drive, from home, get into the car a mere few steps from my door, and have the luxury of being alone for the drive to Counties Limerick and Clare, to meet the writer I wish to speak to.

It is completely my choice that I elect to go by the only slightly less convenient method of public transport, drawing out my journey for as long a duration as possible. This is done so as to connect fraternally, if only on a symbolic level, with the Asylum Seeker, who is forced to travel by truly difficult methods, and forces, in truly difficult circumstances. But my journey, by bus and coach will be far from a forced or difficult journey.

By now, in truth, I have become an armchair traveller[8]. Most of this journey has taken place already in my imagination, after all, more so than in reality; and the planning has been greater than, can only be greater than, the actuality.

Alain De Botton writes:

> One question revolves around the relationship between the anticipation of travel and its reality… the reality of travel is not what we anticipate … It may be truer and more rewarding to suggest that it is primarily *different*[9].

The day of the meeting, I walk to the local bus stop a mere five minutes away, catch the bus soon after, and get brought to Cork Bus Station on Parnell Place, early for the Expressway to Limerick.

I have time to kill; then again, I will have time to kill all day, I have all the time in the world, for mine is a slight journey of 120 kilometres; I will be home by dinner-time, I will return to my own house, eat at my own table, I will sleep in my own bed, I will be with who is familiar to me.

There is neither fear nor trepidation associated with this upcoming journey, because I can picture in my mind each stage, and how it will conclude. I am leaving nothing permanently behind and I will be returning to everything I possess. There are no losses in my journey; and there is restoration of everything and anything left behind. I go from, and return to, home.

Direct Provision Centres, I am conscious as I consider them, are not 'home'; they are public places put into use for private living, often forcing the private into

---

8 Coverly, above cite, p20.

9 Alain De Botton, *The Art of Travel*, London, 2014, pp9-12.

the public. The role of home is imposed upon them, and there is little room for true privacy.

My home is and will remain a home; on leaving, on return.

How fortunate I am: in a familiar place, with those familiar to me nearby.

Standing in line for the Limerick bus in Cork Bus Station, I suddenly can see that I should not go to visit or see Knockalisheen Accommodation Centre.

For the true purpose of this trip, it is apparent to me now, and an important part, is not to go there, but rather to go and meet my mentee and discuss her writing, and to hear, in her own words, of her journey from Zimbabwe to Ireland and of her life here. Yes, to listen, and to assist, to go and make a gesture of fraternity and connection, and not merely on a symbolic level.

But to go to Knockalisheen Accommodation Centre would be more than merely an inessential journey. It would be a potentially intrusive one, imposing on another's privacy.

At that moment, I resolve not to go there, but to meet my mentee where we have initially elected to meet, in Limerick Bus Station.

The bus pulls in to the station and the subsequent journey I take is uneventful: ninety minutes from Cork through Mallow, Buttevant, Ballyhea, Charleville, Rourkes Cross, and thence to Limerick.

We meet in the station café.

We talk, writer to writer, mentor to mentee, and I hear her story of how she got from Zimbabwe to Ireland in her own words, and her experience of living here.

This is an essential journey.

## Photography

BY VUKAŠIN NEDELJKOVIĆ

Old Convent Direct Provision Centre, Ballyhaunis

Old Convent Direct Provision Centre, Ballyhaunis

Old Convent Direct Provision Centre, Ballyhaunis

## In The Irish Countryside

BY DAVE LORDAN

In the Irish countryside
in places few people live

on their way to &
inside the slaughterhouse

cattle bellow for help
like industrial children

who can be heard for miles
who can be heard for centuries.

Some tourist or artist or hiker
passing through
may pause

and go pale
at the screeching terror of it

but no-one ever answers the call –
its meaning so obvious

no-one ever goes to their aid.

******

Humans could never form without our enshrouding numbness, our skin.

The skin is precisely that thin nerveless layer which is both inside and outside of us and which feels nothing.

Without skin every instant would be unbearable torture. A raindrop would scald and a rain shower cause an incredible agony.

Mosquitos would envelop us like a living net and drain our blood vessels completely.

Similarly the psyche has its thin protective layer of numbness or 'Ice' as Kafka calls it, which feels nothing and thus protects us from bottomless sorrow and horror we are everywhere surrounded with.

How shall we ever get through it?

*****

In bed listening to the wind. Imagining a gull helplessly hithered and thithered by the wind. Imagining my life as a gull in the wind. Wanting to let go, to go with the wind.

*****

At the 25th hour<br>
on the 32nd of July<br>
on the 33rd county<br>
on Planet B<br>
children will have nothing to fear<br>
and grown-ups will be free

*****

Wet shimmering black brickwork, glaring electric light, endless dark of the universe.

*****

At the end of June 1970, fellow child inmates witnessed William being beaten with a broomstick by a Christian Brother, beaten until he was knocked into unconsciousness. I invite you now to imagine the sight – & the sounds & the smells & perhaps also the tastes, yes the whole sensorium – of a man beating a child with a broomstick until the child's brain shuts down.

*****

Investors and developers are the true creative spirits of this world. They are the ones who transform the world in the image of their own desires. Artists are only a parody of them.

******

With relish & triumph, the mouse downed the slug. The hedgehog devoured the mouse. The rat left not a molecule behind of the hedgehog. The fox inhaled the rat. The boar made fast food of the fox. The man shot the boar. Which made a fair few fleas homeless. Briefly, for they soon alighted on the man, who had a long full beard & a lovely hairy back for them to settle snugly into. They felt like they had moved just like that from a hovel to a mansion – rags to riches in one glorious instant! But that didn't last long either, for the man barbecued the boar for his birthday a few days layer & fed it in chops & burgers to a long line of family & friends & then he died along with all the rest of them from a virus passed on from the slug & so the fleas moved on & so did the virus & that's not the end of it either. Oh no it isn't!

*****

*As distant in time from the Greek and Roman eras as we are today, the Bronze Age is certainly buried in the pre-modern. But as we think our present-day, modern thoughts, how different are they, really, from those thoughts in the first, Bronze Age civilizations? How many deep habits of mind, institutions, routines, go back to the Bronze Age and its brand-new spirit and ethos? Was that not the origin of the notion, so basically corrosive to autonomy and freedom, that inequality and hierarchy are normal conditions and that misfortune is not a social evil but an individual's just deserts?*

John Zerzan

*****

We have as much chance of being able to stand objectively outside our lives to find out what they mean as the words in a book do of reading themselves out loud.

*****

*In those late wars in Munster; for notwithstanding that the same was a most rich and plentiful country, full of corn and cattle, that you would have thought they could have been able to stand long, yet ere one year and a half they were brought to such wretchedness, as that any stony heart would have rued the same. Out of every corner of the wood and glens they came creeping forth upon their hands, for their legs could not bear them; they looked Anatomies of death, they spoke like ghosts, crying out of their graves; they did eat of the carrions corpses, happy where they could find them, yea, and one another soon after, in so much as the very carcasses they spared not to scrape out of their graves; and if they found a plot of water-cresses or shamrocks, their they flocked as to a feast for the time, yet not able long to continue therewithal; that in a short space there were none almost left, and a most populous and plentiful country suddenly left void of man or beast.*

Edmund Spenser

*****

What we do unto the othered shall be done unto us, times over.

&

what I lately realised is this:
that the first plough tore up the earth for good.

That Schöningen's thrusting spears
destroyed Hiroshima
400,000 years ago.

That there is no going back &
it's getting worse, far worse,
before it gets worse

and
that I have nothing to offer
but these windows unto doom,
more of it.

*****

*"There is no happiness like that of being loved by your fellow creatures, and feeling that your presence is an addition to their comfort."*
— Charlotte Brontë, *Jane Eyre*

*****

Inside us, a sleeping God is trying to arise.
But we are the also the Devil's ark.
Human actions are either angelic – God-awakening,
or demonic, calling the devil awake.

# An Emergency in Direct Provision

BY CÓNAL THOMAS

Take the M50 from Dublin and head on to the M1. Drive for over an hour until you reach the small town of Carrickmacross in Co. Monaghan. Pass through the main street and follow the R179 for 5 kilometres until you reach Treacy's Hotel.

Last September, asylum seekers who'd recently arrived in Ireland were placed at Treacy's by The Department of Justice & Equality's Reception and Integration Agency (RIA), which administers Ireland's direct provision system.

Criticised for the length of time people remain in centres while their asylum applications or appeals are processed, the remote locations of centres as well as the psychological effects on those living in them, Direct Provision Centres are generally re-purposed or purpose-built facilities to accommodate asylum seekers who arrive in Ireland. Implemented in 1999, over 6,000 people live in direct provision.

Some centres are state-run but most are tendered out to private contractors. Payments to private companies totalled €72 million last year.

Yet Ireland's direct provision system is at capacity.

It started with five hotels and B&Bs dotted around Cavan-Monaghan. By December, six hotels and B&Bs were contracted by RIA to provide emergency accommodation for asylum seekers. By February, this number had risen to 11 hotels and B&Bs.

There are now over 1,000 people living in 30 emergency accommodation centres open in 12 counties around Ireland.

...

Relocations soon became commonplace for those placed in emergency accommodation.

On Thursday 7th March, 100 asylum seekers living at Treacy's Hotel were relocated to a hotel in the small village of Laytown, Co. Meath. Others were dispersed to B&Bs in Co. Monaghan. Several others to a hotel in Co. Louth.

The difference for the 1,035 people residing in hotels and B&Bs and people in Ireland's 39 Direct Provision Centres? Service provision.

Since September, complaints have been made to RIA about the type of food being served at hotels, of no access to GP services, no access to medical cards for more than eight months, local GP practices not accepting people as patients without medical cards, delays in PPS numbers being allocated in order to receive weekly payment of €38.80, a lack of educational access for children and unsuitable accommodation.

More recently, a lack of oversight of these private businesses has been highlighted while a lack of vulnerability assessments for people entering the country before being moved to a hotel or B&B has been of growing concern.

RIA aims to open new Direct Provision Centres. Yet recent arson attacks at a hotel in Moville, Co Donegal and at the Shannon Key West Hotel in Roosky, Co Leitrim put paid to plans for added DP stock. The Department of Justice & Equality has now paid €9 million to private business owners operating emergency accommodation set-ups in the past 12 months. On average, businesses are paid €100 per night per bed.

...

Meanwhile, our Justice Department struggles to maintain even existing direct provision stock.

In July, Hatch Hall in Dublin city centre was closed to be redeveloped as a five-star hotel. Asylum seekers, many of whom had lived at Hatch Hall for years, were moved to Balseskin Reception Centre in Dublin, an asylum seeker's first port-of-call upon arrival in Ireland before transfer to a Direct Provision Centre where they live – possibly for years – awaiting a decision on their asylum claim.

Balseskin, primarily an assessment centre, is now at capacity, too.

As emergency accommodation became entrenched, no training is being put in place for staff working at hotels and B&Bs. Or, in other words, private businesses RIA has no oversight of.

Staff hold clinics with residents in emergency accommodation to address concerns. Yet RIA also has no official role in carrying out inspections of emergency accommodation set-ups nor can it permit visits – unlike permanent Direct Provision Centres.

RIA knows it can't cope with this pressure. It recently asked NGOs to help by introducing a "Cultural Liaison Service" to assist people living in emergency conditions.

A mother, who fled Zimbabwe with her teenage son in January, hoping to enroll him in secondary school. A man moved three times in 9 months from one remote location to the next. An infant left without baby formula. The 15 hours between meal times in a Dublin hotel.

Or the overcrowded rooms in a Roscrea hostel. Families washing their clothes in hotel sinks for six months. Residents in a Bray hotel told they're not allowed visitors. A 10pm curfew imposed at a Co. Clare hostel.

...

In June, retired High Court Judge Dr Bryan McMahon, who chaired 2015's working group report into the direct provision system, said he was 'totally against' the use of emergency accommodation for international protection applicants and called on RIA to expand its stock by building on State-owned sites.

Three days beforehand, Deputy Secretary General Oonagh Buckley of the Justice Department told an Oireachtas Committee that emergency set-ups are of a lower standard that Direct Provision Centres.

The same standards provided in Direct Provision Centres, she said, can't be provided for the 1,070 people now residing in hotels and B&Bs.

Last year, Ireland signed up to EU Reception Conditions directive.

The directive states that the Minister may provide emergency accommodation. But it must be for "as short a time as possible".

Ireland is also legally required to conduct vulnerability assessments, which aim to identify special reception needs for asylum seekers and refugees. These, too, are not taking place.

...

RIA aims to end its use of emergency accommodation by late 2019. For now, people remain in hotels and B&Bs living alongside Ireland's homeless.

Did planning go into addressing this rise in numbers of people applying for international protection in Ireland?

RIA could not foresee two arson attacks at planned Direct Provision Centres. Yet in 2015, McMahon's report predicted asylum applications would increase 100% by 2019. This was not unforeseen. What did our Justice Department expect to happen?

During this period, NGOs like Nasc and Irish Refugee Council, have been quick to note that the number of international protection applicants entering Ireland remains at manageable levels.

Yet faced with rising far-right sentiment, public procurement issues, difficulties in direct provision residents finding suitable accommodation in the rental sector once granted leave-to-remain, RIA relies on our private market to provide.

Despite saying in early January that international protection applicants are placed in emergency accommodation "for a short period before they are moved into the mainstream accommodation system", only 285 people have been moved to Direct Provision Centres.

## Up The Hill In Mayo

BY OWODUNNI MUSTAPHA

Safely tucked into my yellow wrapper,
strapped to my back is my nine-month-old baby
with luggage dragged along
and my two little fellas running behind me.

We're in Dublin,
the hustle and bustle like Lagos.
Dublin buses remind me of BRT buses in Lagos,
the magnificent GPO resembles the Cathedral on Marina Street,
the long stretch of O'Connell Street reminds me of Oshodi,
everyone in a hurry as if they were at Lagos Island Market.
I feel at ease but it isn't home.

As we embark on a seemingly endless journey to Mayo,
I notice the excitement on the kids' faces,
the thrill in their voices as the bus descends the bridge,
their amazement at the train tracks, the smell of the countryside,
the sight of cows and sheep, the peace and quiet.

The sight of a ginormous building jolts me back to reality –
we arrive like a 'Johnny Just Come'.
Up the hill we go.
Gates close behind us.
Is this ancient building home?

Life up the hill is turbulent –
tension between neighbours,
the anger I feel when the kids refer to the town centre as 'down the hill' or 'down the road'.
How do I help the kids feel they belong in the community and not behind the gate?

I heave a sigh of relief when I to go to Castlebar,
the green landscape on Westport road and mountain views,
the picturesque surroundings of Westport House
and the quintessential reverence of Croagh Patrick,
how I bask in the euphoria of Knock shrine!

The journey to asylum seems endless;
all you can do is persevere and be hopeful
when you live up the hill in Mayo.

## Managua to Finglas

BY JANE CLARKE

She gives us her city in pictures,
yellow hammocks among palm trees,

night blooming cactus, pine-needle
baskets of plantains ripening in the heat.

She's at her Huembes Market stall
from dawn, selling fresh-cut guavas,

cherimoyas, papaya and lime.
Elena, Luisa, Maribel, her daughters

in navy tunics and white ankle socks,
spick and span as morning, saunter

past the corner shop to school.
That was before protesters

bled in the streets, before
teenagers assassinated by police,

before the gun pressed into her back,
a message hissed in her ear,

before she told the girls it was time
to pack their lives into a rucksack.

## Behind the Wall I Escape

by Deborah Oniah Blankson

Behind the wall of unemployment, I escaped.

I have a right to work. I have a Law Degree and a Life Coaching Certificate. How do I begin? How can I work professionally and who will employ me? Even though I see many barriers ahead, I say yes to every training opportunity that is offered to me. I speak up whenever I have the chance. I have completed intercultural dialogue training to become a facilitator in that area. I am also writing again with Fiction at the Friary. There is no barrier there.

With speaking and writing, I escape.

Behind the wall of staying idle, I escape. I live a life of routine, breakfast, sleep, lunch, sleep and dinner, sleep. Being idle with nothing to do or look forward to and waiting for the Government to say yes is very hard. To move ahead is very hard. Not being able to fully integrate or belong to a group outside the wall of the hostel is very sad, but I escape.

I joined the Sanctuary Runners and the Park Run. Before I came to Ireland in 2018, I never ran in my life, but I did the Cork City Marathon and I finished it. It was one of my greatest achievements. Running, I now have friends. I am very healthy and positive.

With running, I escape.

Behind the wall of the hostel, being in the asylum process, the dreaded brown registered envelope evokes much fear. The fear of uncertainty is very real. I am not sure what the Justice Department will say, or when they will make a decision. In this state, my life and safety and that of my children is one thing that keeps me awake most nights, low some days and full of fear on many other days.

It can eat your time, mind, health and everything that gives you strength, but with nature and the people I met everyday, I escape.

The air that I breathe says yes to me. The green grass and trees say yes to me. The genuine people I have met since being here say yes to me. I know for sure this time my brown registered envelope will say yes to me.

So, with faith, I escape.

Behind the wall of nothing, I escape. Since coming here to Ireland, I know how important it is to seek help and when you get help, to stay committed, not go back. After my intervention since being here, I have said yes to almost every opportunity that has come my way. That is the beauty of Ireland and life in general. It presents you with opportunity and if you have nothing, that opportunity is the something that you can have. I have said yes to the Cork City of Sanctuary Movement, yes to facilitating, yes to continuous learning, yes to being a member of Boards working with asylum seekers and yes to speaking and I will say yes to many more opportunities that I have.

So, behind the wall of nothing, by saying yes, I have escaped.

# Winter Song Of The Guardian

by Theo Dorgan

The snow came sweeping down through the dark wood,
the tree-tops clear above the driving snow,
I climbed to where the house of night still stood,
the path my mother climbed so long ago.

The path my father made so long ago,
the house he built where once a broad oak stood,
the tree that fell beneath a weight of snow
and gave him these great beams of time-dark wood.

Their voices echo down the deep of time,
sweep past me through the wood and down the hill.
How many souls have made this heavy climb,
how many are they who must make it still?

How many are there who must make it still,
put down their burdens, face into this climb
that leads to the bright stars above the hill,
the vault of heaven overarching time?

The vault of heaven stands above the roof.
I light a fire inside, throw wide the door,
I let the blaze shine out as living proof
my people keep their bargain with the poor.

My people keep their bargain with the poor,
this fire at heart of winter living proof:
Once we were made the keepers of the door,
all are made welcome under this wide roof.

# What's in a Name?

BY REHAN ALI

It's the wind. No more *Samurai Jack*. Only pixels of black and white, dancing in a relentless pattern on the screen. No more cartoons. What to do now? Where to go? Oh, it will be another boring summer day in Bridgewater House.

The subdued light from the clouded sky glowed through the cracked glass. Better than no light. The window opened with a struggle. A fresh breeze crept in. My hand reached out at the wall that swarmed with rusted satellites. A collection of black and bronze unblinking eyes. I felt the rough mesh with my fingertips. Pulled it towards me. It has to face eastwards. The perfect angle. Did it work? A quick twist of my neck towards the buzzing screen says no. 'Hmm…, maybe if I do this?' No, still not working. But the view wasn't all bad, I guess. I could see the New Bridge. Traffic lights. Cars. Trucks. Bikes. And people. But I was looking from underneath, half veiled and half breathing. I am under.

'How many times do I have to tell you?' She walked in yelling. I had been told before of the dangers of falling. Although landing was really the dangerous part. I pulled away with a sigh, the window closed off the world once more. 'But what about my cartoons?' After all every ten year old child watched cartoons. So I couldn't be that different. 'You will have to do something else.' But what? I guess I could roam the hostel, see what I could find. Perhaps a friend.

Best friends, I had so many. Reza from Iran, Ose from Nigeria, Roman from Russia, Chechnya, China, Kenya, Iraq. This was the brief window of time where I had none. They would come and go, I would remain. Ten years. Solitude, confined. I was part of the world and yet not. Wandering from floor to floor. How many paintings on the walls? 28, for sure. One had a gold frame, and a bowl placed by the edge, like me on the window sill. I've become familiar with the edge, as has my mother.

She wanted to give us the open sky and unfolded sea. To blaze a trail so we could succeed. The mail that had been left for her had different intentions. I had seen it earlier, by her bedside. Brown and large. I've always known, I guess, that there was something to be feared. I can feel it coming. Although my eyes are shut tight by the force of childhood, I can still sense it. Yes, it's here. And much like the weather, she couldn't quite keep it together. She's been losing sleep and I've been keeping myself awake. I can sense her thoughts. 'Can I make it before I lose my mind? Who chooses what stays and what fades away? We need a revelation. It's time to pray. The old remedy. But it's a prayer I can't complete tonight. Where do we go from here? Self-serving prayers only go so far.'

'Why do you live there? What is it?' Questions I've heard growing up. We're sewn into the landscape, can't you see? How can we return now? The pressure of heavy choices. You want to get it, right? But you don't understand the violence of a choice. And all we are, are choices not a thousand different faces. My history is etched into documents. My life simplified into black and white. It wasn't enough? How long before I am released from behind these walls? I want my future. You can make do with my past. I need the day, I'm growing tired of this night. But still I remain nameless. Like the others. 'What's in a name?' you ask. I wish to be named.

Call me whatever you want. Anything you want. Tell me what you want me to be. As long as freedom accompanies your calls. This place is a house, but this soil is a home. And it is where we need to exist. We can't leave now. And go where? Land over land, blood over sand. What a place to come from. Will we really no longer be able to stay? Much like the river Suir under the New Bridge, my mind runs free. But will it drown me? A fantasy of a world not overgrown, a world of compassion and promise remains fantasy after all. Will we drown?

But there's plutonium in our veins. Don't come too close, we might explode. A volatile group. Kept away, atoms apart. Our ambition, a complex equation. Our hope, a catalyst. There's nothing quite like this. Our love, the purest element. Can you feel it? Our half-life, a quarter of yours. Oxidised by a stranger air. Will we always be afraid? Or is it we who are feared. Risk it all for one bright spark. Let our chemicals spill. Let our fumes dissolve. Born out of the earth, soil darker than yours. Breaking down again, although the barriers are lasting. And you simply can't get enough. More, more, more, just not enough.

But this is a good place to fall. What do I choose? At the end of the road, when there's no more hope. I choose me. I choose us. I am young. So let us fall, but let us restart.

# Endless Summer

BY IAN MALENEY

I spent my summer days in my grandmother's house. Curtains drawn to hide the boring, endless sun. Stealing sweets from the bowl on top of the fridge, once we were tall enough to reach. I don't remember when *Dino Babies* and *Rugrats* became *Murder, She Wrote* and *Columbo* – sometime in the afternoon, thirteen, fourteen years old. From cartoons to murder mysteries, all in the sticky half-dark of the unchanging sitting room.

Of course we were forced out eventually. Someone in authority would arrive and say enough was enough, and kick us into the sunshine. The middle of nowhere in the middle of the year; long days, long hours, not a bloody thing to do. No friends around when school was out, just little brothers and occasional cousins. I thought I knew boredom, but maybe not. I took the space for granted; I explored, unsupervised, a few square miles of unfenced playground, green and soft and empty. The narrow streams, the landmark rocks, the squat sparse trees – I knew them all by heart for a time at least. What a place to come from.

Stuffed with the skater dreams of suburban American kids but surrounded by grass and gravel, we made our own equivalents of the quarter-pipes and rails we saw on television. Anything you could throw yourself off, with a board, bike, or blades. We were industrious and, in our own minds, fearless. Bony young bodies in flight, for a second or two at least, as the wheels left the plywood boards balanced on an upturned wheelbarrow and soared through the empty air above the hill before crashing inelegantly onto the flat grass below. Success was getting back up and trying again. Nothing broken but much bruised, landing was always the dangerous part.

It wasn't that long ago. Back then I thought everyone survived those July and August days in this vacant, fumbling way. They didn't though, and they don't. What an odd kind of freedom we had – nothing to do and no one to stop us; free to roam with nothing to see. We knew everyone in the houses up and down the road, and they knew us. Such-and-such's son, such-and-such's grandson – the palpable air of continuity enveloping us, giving us roots and a sense of belonging.

For years, decades even, I never had a question asked of me that wasn't, *And whose son are you?* Crossing fields that belonged to strangers, cycling roads miles from home, I didn't warrant a second glance. At school, the teachers knew my parents, my aunts, my uncles. I never really had to account for myself or my presence in any given place. I was never an unknown, never suspect, never a threat, because I was a continuation. This is the freedom that belonging brings. And this is what it comes down to, in the end, isn't it? Who faces the inquisition, who gets policed; who gets to jump and fall and land in whatever way they like. Boring summer days and *Samurai Jack* – some of us have that much in common – but freedom is something else.

# The Welcoming Project

BY CATHERINE YOUNG

'It takes a village"

Photo: Ray Hegarty

I began working with people in direct provision in 2016. Having emigrated to America myself, living there for 8 years, I knew first-hand how it was to leave your whole life behind, family and friends and start over somewhere else. I wasn't fleeing war or persecution, I spoke English and was eligible to work in the US, and still it was hard. I could only imagine what it would be like to arrive somewhere, not speak the language well, not to be allowed work, to be of a very different culture to the place where you've arrived and alongside that, be dealing with your own personal trauma of what you might have gone through. Then to be hidden away, often on the peripheries of Irish towns and forgotten about…

I had wanted for some time to try to use dance and music as a way to bring people from different cultures together and in 2016 when asked to create a new dance work for Féile Fáilte as part of The Casement Project by Féarghus O'Conchúir, I decided to try. Getting access to the centres was not always so easy but I was relentless and spent weeks trying to build connections and find ways in (which often involved playing hours of badminton and ping pong at Tralee International Resource Centre). The idea was to provide a safe space where people from all backgrounds could come together and share their culture – their music, dance and singing. Not having English wouldn't be an issue as dance is language beyond words and connects people through the physicality of the human body. Participants were invited to learn all styles – African dance, Irish dance, Palestinian/Syrian Dabke, Pakistani dance, contemporary dance. Whatever styles participants had to share were woven into the fabric of the sessions. At the outset of the project, many of the bodies in the room felt repressed, stifled, but as the project progressed people began to slowly open up. Learning and embodying someone else's culture allows for an embodied understanding of the other and brings people together in a very real way. There is immense power in the physical act of touching - holding hands with someone you might never connect with outside the studio.

The goal for the project has always been a mix 50:50 of locals to asylum seekers/refugees/migrants – a place outside of the centres (which have mainly been theatre spaces: Siamsa Tire & Backstage Theatre) where people can come together and dance. There are so few opportunities for us to meet our new neighbors and connect, especially with those in direct provision and many of these cultures do not revolve around a pub culture, many don't have the financial resources to socialise and some don't have adequate language skills or are simply afraid. Music and dance cut through all this and bring out the best in people. Through the dance project, people take to the stage empowered and strong and not as victims. Over the past 3 years we have created 3 large scale dance works together: 'Welcoming the Stranger' (2016), 'It takes a village' (2017), 'Le Chéile' (2019). Participants hail from every inch of the globe: Iraq, Syria, Palestine, Afghanistan, Pakistan, Saudi Arabia, Zimbabwe, Malawi, Congo, Kenya, South Africa, Ethiopia, Somalia, Nicaragua, Bangladesh to name but a few. The journey in creating these pieces, has transformed the group into a second family of sorts – where love, respect, kindness, equality and hospitality are abundant. It is not only the asylum seekers who benefit. Local communities have spoken of how important this community has become in their lives. In a world where technology has taken us further away from 'physical' community, *The Welcoming Project* brings people physically back together. In the rehearsal room, everyone is equal, the energy is positive, upbeat, joyful. Rehearsals offer people respite, a break from the monotony and boredom of life in direct provision, a space where people can re-connect to themselves, to their bodies and with each other, somewhere to find a bit of freedom and feel good about themselves.

But not everyone wants to perform – so in 2018, we opened up the project further to allow everyone access. In a nod to the céilí dances of old, we ran our first CÉILÍ AFRO DABKE – a world music céilí, encompassing African dance, Dabke and the traditional Irish céilí dances. Instead of performing our shows in theatres, we took the shows from the stage to community halls and opened up the space after each performance, to allow everyone join in and dance together.

While the shows offer a vision of how things 'could' be and empower participants on stage, the reality for those in direct provision is far from this. Some residents asked about addressing their issues in the shows, others felt that if they spoke out it would negatively impact their cases and make their lives more difficult and were fearful. But all agreed that a show needed to be made around these issues and so STATE OF EXCEPTION was created in 2018. This work attempts to show the impact of direct provision on the human body: the isolation, the boredom, the endless waiting, the eroding of one's dignity, and the fight to maintain one's physical and mental health through it all. The show stresses the solution to all of this comes through **us**. We know this is going on and we have the opportunity to do something, to be a voice and a vote for those that have none. Despite challenges, there is always something we can do, with whatever skills we have to make their situation a little easier while we ask for a dismantling of this system. Can we engage, interact, seek out the other and make them feel more welcome and part of our community? In my own personal experience and I know I speak also for all involved in the dance project, the people we have met have become our friends, our extended family and have enriched our lives in an extraordinary way. They have taught us much about joy, resilience, love and the power of community and coming together. In Ireland, we need these new communities as much as they need us to remind us of what's important, so we all can prosper.

*The Welcoming Project is currently supported by: Kerry County Council, the Arts Council, Creative Ireland & Siamsa Tire. Prior projects supported by: Backstage Theatre, Longford County Council, Shawbrook dance & Dept. of Justice "Integration Funds."*

## Scars

BY NOKUKHANYA DLAMINI

They might be physical,
they might be emotional,
but they are scars.

Not talking or showing them
is my way of moving on.
Revisiting those events and emotions
is a torture I decided
to bury.

How many more times
do I have to tell the buried scar
for you to believe?

I need to show no proof
to show I have emotional scars –
but it doesn't mean
they are not there.

Physical scars heal,
sometimes they even leave no mark.
But emotional scars
are always raw –

anything touches them,
they bleed.
Their wound does not heal easily.
Not seeing them doesn't mean
they are not there.

You learn to live with them.
You learn ways
of not touching and wounding them.

You learn to move on
and live happily with them.
After all, they are scars.

## Scalpel

BY JESSICA TRAYNOR

My only visible scar
the pale ridge on my thigh
where the doctor grasped
the ink-black freckle
in the months after childbirth
and sent me for a biopsy.

Now nothing left
except this jagged little knife-kiss,
raised and clumped
like milk teeth pushing
through gum

because I am lucky enough
to live in a country
where any
small
inconvenience
is
quickly
(quietly)

removed.

# Biographies

**Anonymous (author of I Had to Keep On)**
The author is originally from Afghanistan, but does not want to detail the particulars of their identity or current location.

**Anonymous (author of Because Justice Matters)**
The author is originally from Zimbabwe, but does not wish to disclose their identity. The writer has been living in Ireland for over ten years and she has a strong interest in human rights.

**Heidar Al-Hashimi**
Alongside his photography, Heidar Al-Hashimi is a Social Researcher and Community Development Worker from Iraq and living in Ireland since 2009. He has an MA in Family Support Studies from NUI Galway, Diploma in Community Development practice from National University of Ireland Galway and Diploma in Community and Family Studies with the same University. He has fluent English and Arabic languages.

**Rehan Ali**
Rehan was born in the city of Rawalpindi, Pakistan. At the age of six, his mother fled the country, taking he and his siblings to the land they would come to know as Ireland. He spent his childhood in a hostel named Bridgewater House in Carrick-on-Suir, Tipperary.

**Nngcobo Bongamahlub**
Nkosikhona Ngcobo is a South African born designer, artist, photographer, writer and social activist who hails from Easterborn Farm in Newcastle kwaZulu-Natal. Growing up in a hometown where culture is abundant and the sense of community is strong, she developed a keen interest in and was ultimately taken by social issues.

**Dr Angela Byrne**
Dr Angela Byrne is a historian specialising in migration and women's history. She is Research Associate at Ulster University and, in 2018-19, is the inaugural DFAT Historian-in-Residence at EPIC The Irish Emigration Museum. She is author of Geographies of the Romantic North (Palgrave Macmillan, 2013), A Scientific, Antiquarian and Picturesque Tour: John (Fiott) Lee in Ireland, England and Wales,

1806–1807 (Routledge for Hakluyt Society, 2018), and many articles and book chapters on the histories of travel and exploration, the Irish abroad, and women in the sciences. She has previously held lecturing and research positions in University of Toronto, University of Greenwich, Maynooth University, and the Royal Irish Academy, as well as visiting fellowships at Cambridge University, the All-Russia State Library for Foreign Literature (Moscow), and the Huntington Library (Los Angeles). Her research is concerned with cross-cultural encounters and the experiences of women and migrants in the past.

**Eileen Casey**

Based in South Dublin, poetry and prose collections are published by Arlen House, AltEnts and New Island. Literary prizes include The Hennessy Emerging Fiction Award and a Patrick and Katherine Kavanagh Fellowship. In 2008, she edited 'Flavours of Home', a combination of recipe/memory of home. This publication gives voice to women living in Direct Provision, Clondalkin at that particular time.

**Sarah Clancy**

Sarah Clancy is a page and performance poet from Galway. She has three collections: Stacey and the Mechanical Bull (Lapwing Press, Belfast, 2011), Thanks for Nothing, Hippies (Salmon Poetry, 2012), and The Truth and Other Stories (Salmon Poetry, 2014). Along with fellow Galway poet Elaine Feeney she released a poetry CD called Cinderella Backwards in 2013. She is frequently invited to read her work at various festivals and events around Ireland and abroad and can't believe she's still getting away with it. She is on twitter @sarahmaintains

**Jane Clarke**

Jane Clarke's first collection, *The River,* was published by Bloodaxe Books in 2015. Her second collection, *When the Tree Falls,* will be published by Bloodaxe Books in September 2019. *All the Way Home,* an illustrated sequence of poems in response to a family archive of First World War photographs and letters held in the Mary Evans Picture Library, London, was published by Smith|Doorstop in April 2019. Originally from a farm in Roscommon, Jane now lives in Glenmalure, Co. Wicklow. In 2016 she won the Hennessy Literary Award for Emerging Poetry with three poems from *The River.* She also won the inaugural Listowel Writers' Week Poem of the Year at the Irish Book Awards. *The River* was shortlisted for the Royal Society for Literature Ondaatje Award, given for a distinguished work of fiction or non-fiction evoking the spirit of a place.

**Katie Donovan**

Katie Donovan was born in 1962 and spent her youth on a farm near Camolin in Co. Wexford. She studied at Trinity College Dublin and at the University of California at Berkeley. She was Writer-in-Residence for Dun Laoghaire/Rathdown 2006-8 and has taught many courses (in Media and Contemporary Irish Literature as well as Creative Writing) in IADT Dun Laoghaire (2006-13). She was a lecturer in Creative Writing, with a focus on poetry, in NUI Maynooth 2015-17. She has published five books of poetry, all with Bloodaxe Books, UK. Her most recent, "Off-Duty" appeared in September 2016. It was shortlisted for the Irish Times/ Poetry Now Prize, 2017. She is the 2017 recipient of the O'Shaughnessy Award for Irish Poetry. She is co-editor, with Brendan Kennelly and A. Norman Jeffares, of the anthology, "Ireland's Women: Writings Past and Present" (Gill and Macmillan, Ireland; Kyle Cathie, UK, 1994; Norton & Norton, US, 1996). She is the author of "Irish Women Writers: Marginalised by Whom?" (Raven Arts Press, 1988, 1991). With Brendan Kennelly she is the co-editor of "Dublines" (Bloodaxe, 1996), an anthology of writings about Dublin. Her poems have appeared in numerous periodicals and anthologies in Ireland, the UK and the US, notably the bestselling "Staying Alive: real poems for unreal times" edited by Neil Astley, and "The Wake Forest Book of Irish Women's Poetry" edited by Peggy O'Brien.

**Theo Dorgan**

Theo Dorgan (born 1953) is an Irish poet, writer and lecturer, translator, librettist and documentary screenwriter. He was educated in North Monastery School. He completed a BA in English and Philosophy and a MA in English at University College Cork, after which he tutored and lectured in that University, while simultaneously Literature Officer with Triskel Arts Centre in Cork. He was visiting faculty at University of Southern Maine. Among his awards are the Listowel Prize for Poetry, 1992 and the O'Shaughnessy Prize for Irish Poetry 2010. A member of Aosdána, he was appointed to The Arts Council / An Chomhairle Ealaíon in 2003. He also served on the Board of Cork European Capital of Culture 2005. He was also awarded the 2015 Poetry Now Award for Nine Bright Shiners. He currently lives in Dublin with his partner, the poet and playwright Paula Meehan.

**Nokukhanya Dlamini**

I am from South Africa. I am a single mother to 4 boys and a little girl. I showed interest in reading books at an early age, I was a great story teller. My family used to gather around and listen to my stories. I had a scribbling book that I wrote many poems to. One of the poems that I wrote was read at my mum's funeral in 2007.

Most of the poems I wrote are about life journey and those who are around me.

**Elaine Feeney**

Elaine Feeney was born in the West of Ireland and lives in Athenry. She published her first chapbook, Indiscipline in 2007, and has since published three collections of poetry, *Where's Katie?* (2010), *The Radio Was Gospel* (2014) and *Rise* (2017) with Salmon Publishing. Feeney was commissioned in 2016 to write a national screen and stage piece, WRoNGHEADED by the Liz Roche Company, which has toured internationally since its first run at Tiger Dublin Fringe Festival. She was Poetry Ireland's Poetry Ambassador in 2018. She teaches English & History at St. Jarlath's College for Boys, Tuam, Creative Writing & Poetry at the National University of Ireland, Galway and she is the Creative Director of the Tuam Oral History Project at the same university, working with survivors of the Tuam Mother and Baby Home to archive their narrative. Feeney's debut novel, *As You Were*, will be published by Harvill Secker/ Penguin Random House in February 2020. She will guest edit The Stinging Fly in 2020. Feeney is agented by Peter Straus at Rogers, Coleridge and White in London.

**Donatien Francis Sibomana**

Donatien was born on the 19th August 1995 in Bujumbura, Burundi. Since coming to Ireland in 2015, he has lived in Mosney Accommodation Centre, Atlantic House in Tramore, and Birchwood House in Waterford.

**Claire Hennessy**

Claire Hennessy is a writer, editor, book reviewer, and creative writing teacher based in Dublin, Ireland. She has written several books for teenagers, and regularly delivers author visits and writing workshops for schools, libraries and festivals. Claire's most recent YA novels *Like Other Girls* and *Nothing Tastes As Good* are published by Hot Key Books. Her work has been nominated for the Irish Book Awards and the Carnegie Medal. Her short fiction has most recently appeared in *Reading The Future* (Arlen House) and *Autonomy* (New Binary Press), and she is the 2015 recipient of the Doolin Short Story Prize. She has received three Arts Council bursaries (for both short fiction and YA) and holds masters' degrees in both Popular Literature and Creative Writing (TCD). She reviews YA fiction for *The Irish Times* and occasionally elsewhere. Claire is a co-director and co-founder of the Big Smoke Writing Factory creative writing school in Dublin, and co-founder and co-editor at *Banshee*, a literary journal and small independent press. She is powered mostly by tea. Claire is represented by Sallyanne Sweeney at MMBcreative.

**Hina Khan**

Hina Khan's work is the constant search for the best way to interpret ideas and express ideologies through symbolism. She has completed her MFA (Masters in

Fine Arts) from FJWU (Fatima Jinnah Women University), Pakistan in 2003, with Miniature Painting as Major. Using a mixture of traditional and innovative techniques, Hina's work portrays social issues, immigration and humanitarian crisis like prostitution, gender discrimination, restrictions, trauma, child abuse and killing.

Hina has participated in a number of exhibitions in recent years in Dublin, Portlaoise and Mayo. Her Solo Show was also displayed at Ballina Art Center, Mayo in 2018. She is planning her next Solo Show in Co. Laois.

**Dave Lordan**

Dave Lordan is a multimedia writer & community educator from West Cork & one of Ireland's best known left-wing artists/activists. Dave collaborates with a wide range of artists in diverse mediums, including Christy Moore (Song), Bernard Clarke (sound) Mary McEvoy (Theatre), Eamonn Crudden (Short Film), Karl Parkinson (Performance), Rob Doyle (Fiction) & Fionn Ó hAlmhain (poetry video). His non-fiction podcast *The Dead Friends* was published by The Dublin Inquirer in 2018. Late 2019 sees the release of his audiotale, *The Only Real Irish Poet in Dublin*, with a soundscape by Derek Flynn.

www.davelordan.com

**Christodoulos Makris**

Christodoulos Makris has published several books, pamphlets, artists' books and other poetry objects, most recently this is no longer entertainment (Dostoyevsky Wannabe, 2019). The Architecture of Chance (Wurm Press, 2015) was a poetry book of the year for RTÉ Arena and 3:AM Magazine. He is the poetry editor at gorse journal and associated imprint Gorse Editions.

**Mimmie Malaba**

Mimmie is 20 years old and is a spoken word poet. She has been writing for nearly two years now and has performed in many places around Ireland. Her biggest performances were in the National Concert Hall in 2019 as part of This Land, a collaboration with a group of singers, musicians, rappers, poets and performers recently arrived in Ireland, and at Electric Picnic in 2018 as part of KaleidSlam. She is currently studying Pre-Nursing. Mimmie posts poetry on Youtube and Instagram.

**Ian Maleney**

Ian Maleney is a writer based in Dublin. He has written for *The Guardian*, *Esquire*, and *The Dublin Review*, amongst others. A collection of essays, *Minor Monuments*, was published by Tramp Press in 2019. He is the non-fiction editor of *The Stinging Fly*, and founding editor of Fallow Media.

**Paula Meehan**

Paula Meehan was born in 1955 in Dublin where she still lives. She studied at Trinity College, Dublin, and at Eastern Washington University in the U.S. She has received many awards, including the Marten Toonder Award for Literature, The Butler Literary Award for Poetry, the Denis Devlin Memorial Award and the PPI Award for Radio Drama. She has published six collections of poetry, the most recent being Geomantic (Dedalus Press, 2016). A selected volume, entitled Mysteries of the Home, was published in 1996 and reissued by Dedalus in 2013. Her writing for stage includes the plays Mrs Sweeney (1997), Cell (1999), and, for children, Kirkle (1995), The Voyage (1997) and The Wolf of Winter (2003/2004). A collection of her radio plays, Music for Dogs, was published by Dedalus in 2008. Meehan's poetry has been set to music by artists as diverse as the avant-garde composer John Wolf Brennan and the folk singer Christy Moore. She has collaborated throughout her working life with dancers, visual artists and filmmakers. A member of Aosdána, the Irish affiliation of writers and artists, Paula Meehan is a former Ireland Professor of Poetry.

**Bulelani Mfaco**

Bulelani has protested since his high school days when he had to march for textbooks and better school infrastructure. Growing up in an Apartheid ghetto, Khayelitsha in Cape Town, he soon realised that he would have to protest for access to land, adequate housing, health care, and improved policing. He has served on numerous community forums in Khayelitsha including the Khayelitsha Health Forum, Neighbourhood watch, and as a branch secretary for the Democratic Alliance. Bulelani left his native South Africa due to targeted killings of LGBT+ people where he lived and sought protection in Ireland. While living in Direct Provision, Bulelani got involved with MASI - Movement of Asylum Seekers in Ireland where he is campaigning for the right to work for all asylum seekers, to end Direct Provision, and regularisation for undocumented people in Ireland.

**Owodunni Mustapha**

Owodunni Mustapha is also known as Ola. She is Nigerian, a 34-year-old single mum of three. She came to Ireland almost five years ago in the wake of the Boko Haram insurgency which led to loss of lives and properties, which the country is yet to recover from. She studied Political Science and has since found passion in writing short plays and poems. Her experience in Direct Provision also triggered her passion for writing. She currently resides at the Old Convent Accommodation Centre in Ballyhaunis.

**Batur Nadir**

Batur Nadir came to Ireland from Afghanistan in 2004, and spent over three years in Direct Provision (Dublin, Carlow, New Ross). He was ten years old when civil war (a product of the Russian-American war), broke out in Kabul. Aged 14, he fled Kabul's war and drought, took shelter in a refugee camp (built by UNHCR) in Peshawar. Fleeing political repression, he made a perilous journey and landed in Ireland. However, his application for asylum was refused, but later he was granted permission to remain. Batur learnt English in Ireland, and after permission to stay, he attended I.T. Carlow, graduating with BSc (Hons) in Physical Therapy. He specialises in lower back pain. He currently lives in Kilkenny with his Irish wife and daughter, she is eleven years old. He writes about war in Afghanistan from his direct experiences and cross-cultural communications. He is currently writing his memoir and a book on Biomechanical Management of Lower Back Pain.

**Annemarie Ní Churreáin**

Annemarie Ní Churreáin is poet from northwest Donegal. Her publications include Bloodroot (Doire Press, 2017) and Town (The Salvage Press, 2018). Ní Churreáin is the 2019 Commissioned Writer at Templebar Gallery + Studios Dublin and a 2019-20 Writer-In-Residence at National University of Ireland Maynooth. More information from www.studiotwentyfive.com.

**Vukašin Nedeljković**

Vukašin Nedeljković is a visual artist and PhD student at the Centre for Transcultural Research and Media Practice at Dublin Institute of Technology. He initiated the multidisciplinary project, Asylum Archive, to collaborate with asylum seekers, artists, academics, civil society activists and immigration lawyers, amongst others, with a view to creating an interactive documentary cross-platform online resource, critically foregrounding accounts of exile, displacement, trauma and memory. www.asylumarchive.com.

**Deborah Oniah Blankson**

Deborah Oniah is a Nigerian mother of four, a writer, speaker and intercultural dialogue facilitator. She has been in Ireland for almost three years. She has a law degree from her home country, she is also a certified life coach, she is a member of the sub advocacy group Cork City of Sanctuary.

**Emilie Pine**

Emilie Pine is Associate Professor in Modern Drama at UCD, and is author of the No.1 bestseller Notes to Self (Tramp Press). She teaches and supervises student work in the fields of theatre and memory cultures. Emilie is Director of the Irish Memory

Studies Research Network (www.irishmemorystudies.com) and Editor of the Irish University Review and recently edited the Special Issue on Moving Memory: The Dynamics of the Past in Irish Culture. She is PI of the IRC New Horizons major project Industrial Memories, a digital witnessing of the 2009 Report of the Commission to Inquire into Child Abuse (Ryan Report). Emilie has published widely in the fields of theatre and memory studies, including The Politics of Irish Memory: Performing Remembrance in Contemporary Irish Culture, published by Palgrave Macmillan. Her forthcoming book is on the dynamics of witnessing memory and trauma in contemporary international theatre (forthcoming, Indiana University Press). Emilie is a member of the Advisory Board of the international Memory Studies Association and is convenor of the Memory Cloud Project.

**Stephen Rea**

Stephen Rea is one of the foremost actors of his generation, coming to world-wide attention when he was nominated for the Academy Award for Best Actor for Neil Jordan's *The Crying Game* in 1992. Rea has enjoyed acclaim on Irish and international stages. Highlights of his theatrical career include; establishing Field Day Theatre Company with Brian Friel in the 1980s; collaborations with Sam Shephard which saw him star in Sam's directorial début of his play *Geography of a Horse Dreamer* in 1974 and Rea's appearances in *Kicking a Dead Horse* and *Ages of the Moon* both at the Abbey and in New York; his unforgettable performance in Enda Walsh's *Ballyturk* (Landmark Productions & Galway International Arts Festival) and most recently, international critical acclaim on both sides of the Atlantic for his performance in *Cyprus Avenue* (Abbey Theatre & Royal Court Theatre production) which enjoyed a lengthy run in New York last year and the Royal Court in London earlier this year. This career has taken place in tandem with his award winning film and television career. Nominated for an Academy Award for his performance as Fergus in *The Crying Game*, his many film credits include *Breakfast on Pluto, Michael Collins, V for Vendetta, The End of the Affair, Black '47.* On TV Stephen won critical acclaim for his performance in *The Honourable Woman*, which also garnered him a BAFTA award.

**Dr Natasha Remoundou**

Natasha was born and raised in Athens, Greece in 1976. She is a mother of four, an activist, and an academic and has lived in Ireland since 2003. She has also lived in the Middle East. For the past two years, she has been a Mayo InterCultural Action volunteer teacher of English to asylum seekers residing in the Ballyhaunis Direct Provision Centre.

**Stephen Sexton**

Stephen Sexton lives in Belfast. His poems have appeared in *Granta, Poetry London*, and *Best British Poetry 2015*. His pamphlet, *Oils*, was the Poetry Book Society's Winter Pamphlet Choice. He was the winner of the 2016 National Poetry Competition, the recipient of an ACES award from the Arts Council of Northern Ireland, and was awarded an Eric Gregory Prize in 2018. His collection *If All the World and Love Were Young* (Penguin, 2019) is shortlisted for the Forward Prize for First Collections (the Felix Dennis Prize).

**Evgeny Shtorn**

Evgeny Shtorn is a civil society activist, organiser and LGBT researcher from Russia. He worked for years in a leading St Petersburg think tank, the Center for Independent Social Research, while also collaborating with such human-rights NGOs as the Russian LGBT Network and Memorial. In 2018, he was forced to leave Russia and claim asylum. His field of work includes hate crimes against LGBT people, racism and postcolonial theory. As an activist he is now trying to create awareness among Irish LGBT community and organizations about the situation with gender based discrimination in Direct Provision where LGBTI and victims of domestic violence are suffering double isolation. For these purposes, he created a grassroots initiative 'Queer Diaspora' in support of people who are seeking asylum.

**Arnold Thomas Fanning**

Arnold Thomas Fanning is an award-winning writer living in Co. Cork, Ireland. His short stories, articles, and essays have been published in The Dublin Review, Banshee, the Irish Times, Crazyhorse Magazine, The Phoenix Anthology of New Irish Writing, gorse, the Sunday Business Post, Hot Press, Longreads.com, Paper Visual Art Journal, and The Lonely Crowd. His work has also been broadcast on BBC Radio 4 and RTÉ Radio 1, including for Arena and A Living Word. He has been granted several Travel & Training Awards from the Irish Arts Council, was awarded a John Hewitt Society International Summer School Bursary, and in 2017 received an Arts Council Bursary in Literature. His first book, Mind on Fire: A Memoir of Madness and Recovery is published by Penguin Ireland.

**Cónal Thomas**

Cónal Thomas is a Staff Reporter with TheJournal.ie. Since November 2018, his work has focused on Ireland's asylum system. He was City Reporter at Dublin Inquirer from 2015 to 2018.

**Jessica Traynor**

Jessica's debut poetry collection, *Liffey Swim* (Dedalus Press, 2014), was shortlisted for the 2015 Strong/Shine Award. In 2016, it was named one of the best poetry debuts of the past five years on Bustle.com. She's currently under commission by BBC, and also by Music for Galway to write an opera with composer Elaine Agnew for Galway 2020 European Capital of Culture. A choral song cycle, 'An Island Sings', was commissioned by Poetry Ireland and Chamber Choir Ireland and was performed in the National Concert Hall in March 2019. Her second collection, 'The Quick', was published in 2018. She is the 2020 Carlow Writer in Residence, and is the recipient of the 2020 Banagher Public Art Commission. She is an inaugural Creative Fellow at UCD.

**Donnah Vuma**

Donnah is originally from Zimbabwe. Currently, she lives in the direct provision system (Knockalisheen center in Co. Clare) with her three children aged 14, 11 and 9 years old respectively. She is a full-time student at the University of Limerick undertaking a joint honor Bachelor of Arts degree in politics and international relations with sociology as a sanctuary scholarship beneficiary. She has a deep-rooted role in activism, constantly campaigning for the rights of asylum seekers and refugees. She believes that seeking asylum is not a crime but a fundamental human right that should be safeguarded by all nations and that no one should ever be forced to sacrifice their freedom for their safety. She is the co-founder of asylum seeker lead group Movement of Asylum Seekers Ireland (MASI), and the founder of a Limerick-based community group called Every Child is Your Child.

**Adam Wyeth**

Adam Wyeth is an award-winning poet, playwright and essayist. He is the author of two critically acclaimed poetry collections. (*Silent Music*, Highly Commended by the UK's Forward Poetry Prize and *The Art of Dying*, An *Irish Times* Book of the Year.) He is also the author of a book of essays, *The Hidden World of Poetry: Unravelling Celtic Mythology in Contemporary Irish Poetry.* His plays have been performed across Ireland and also in New York and Berlin. Salmon published his play *This Is What Happened* in 2019. He is an Associate Artist of the Civic Theatre, Dublin. The World Premiere of his play *Apartment Block* is currently in development for an Off-Broadway production in New York. He teaches online creative writing at adamwyeth.com and fishpublishing.ie.

**Insaf Yalcinkaya**

Insaf Yalcinkaya is a Kurdish poet from Turkey, and was born 31st July 1972 in Dersim, Turkey. After her Bachelor's degree she started to teach at primary and secondary schools. She was a political activist, also Political Consultancy – advising politicians on local and national issues. She had several times ceramics and art exhibitions. Her articles were published in some national and local magazines and newspapers in Turkey. After she moved to Ireland she started to translate her poems in English. She is still in Direct Provision as an asylum seeker in Ireland. She is a member of Dublin Writer's Forum since September 2017. Also she joined Poetry in The Park Killarney. She read her poems during some poetry events open mic in Dublin and Killarney. For instance, during Kilmainham and Inchicore festival 2017, she read at Poetry Ireland Open Mic at Cabra library, Inchicore Library Open Mic, and at Books Upstairs. At the Lord Edward, she has read at the Sunflower Sessions. She was a member of Killarney Drama Circle and Catherine Young's dance group.

**Catherine Young**

Catherine Young is a Dance Ireland Associate Artist and currently dancer in residence with Kerry County Council/the Arts Council at Siamsa Tire. She has created work for the Dublin Dance Festival, Dublin Fringe Festival, Coiscéim Dance Theatre, The Big Bang Festival of Rhythm, Féile Fáilte and the University of Limerick among others.

www.catherineyoungdance.com

**Marwa Zamir**

Marwa is from Afghanistan and is fifteen years old. She is living in Ballyhaunis Direct Provision Centre.